MW00478427

ADVANCE PRAISE FOR
MARK PETERS AND THE SOURCE

"Through helping establish The SOURCE, Mark Peters has created a framework for executives who are passionate about and desire to invest in the success of their employees that recognizes the critical role employees play in the overall long-term success of companies. The dozens of Western Michigan companies partnering in The SOURCE have long demonstrated that commitment to their people, and it shows in the success of our region. This book explains how to bring similar results to your community and company."

—Doug DeVos, Co-Chairman, Amway

"Riveting and impactful, this book is chock full of practical experience that is translatable to Anytown USA. Determined to find a way to benefit employees, business results, and community, Mark Peters explains how a dysfunctional family relationship led to innovating a whole new way for business to collaborate. This timely book makes it clear that business leaders have the opportunity to make real and lasting improvements in the lives of their employees."

—Fred Keller, Founder and Chair, Cascade Engineering

"Discovering The SOURCE in Grand Rapids felt like finding an oasis in the desert. It brilliantly combines the rigor and accountability of the private sector with the compassion and connection of social services, but without the bureaucracy and stigma. We have learned that when leaders from the private sector take responsibility for the well-being of their community, they provide a CEO function missing in a world that has become siloed by expertise, sectors and jurisdictions. In his book, Mark Peters not only provides the inspiration and a map to transform a community, he provides a blueprint for others to transform their company. What an outstanding example of a civic steward—a leader who embraces the responsibility side of citizenship."

—Deborah Nankivell, CEO, Fresno Business Council

"To quote Mark Peters in his new book, 'If we, as the nation's business leaders, do nothing to meet the challenges faced by the people who come to work for us, we will be victims to an economic and social system gone awry.' Armed with ingenuity and a drive to do business better, Mark forged a model to meet the challenges of people and to strengthen business at the same time. The SOURCE is replicable and effective. An idea made real."

—Kathy Crosby, Past CEO, Goodwill West Michigan;
Board of Trustees, Grand Rapids Community College

"Mark addresses the three fundamental aspects for success in The SOURCE: People, Process and Performance. In this book, he shares what it takes to motivate a person, develop well-defined processes, and lead them to exceptional performance. I have admired his leadership for long and am elated that he has articulated his experiences, so the world now can admire him as well."

—Murthy Kalkura, CEO, 4AM Corp.

"Mark Peters, the long-time CEO of one of Western Michigan's iconic businesses, explains how he and fellow far-sighted business leaders created a collective solution to the problems they all face: absenteeism, turnover, and lack of career path. In The SOURCE, Peters explains how they founded a successful organization, and how you can, too."

—Greg McCann, Founder, McCann and Associates

"Within his book, Mark has laid out a clear path on how to balance the corporate bottom line with community betterment and deliver a story of shared success that remains elusive to most organizations. The SOURCE demonstrates how the power of collaboration can help "little" companies make a big difference, and "big" companies transform the world. At a time when a new social contract is needed, CEOs of even the largest global enterprises may be pleasantly surprised to find that a roadmap to success lies within the pioneering approach of a group of mid-sized companies in Michigan."

—George Hemingway, CEO, Stratalis Group

"Mark Peters doesn't just talk about what employers should do, he is intentional about putting what he writes into practice through his CEO title and his stewardship in the community. He digs deep with personal and professional experiences to back him and is our modern-day proof that businesses can do good and do well."

—Liddy Romero, CEO, WorkLife Partnership

"This is a story about value: valuing people and recognizing the way they can and want to contribute to the business; value for the not-for-profit and public support systems who can much more efficiently and effectively provide services to support people and families who are contributing their best to support themselves and their families; and the value of partnerships that support adaptability, creativity, and integrity. Mark Peters and The SOURCE demonstrate how employers, so often unengaged, can be drivers for change centered on their employees and the community, but with returns on each partners' investment."

—Andrew Brower, Program Officer,
W.K. Kellogg Foundation

"The SOURCE plays a crucial role in the Western Michigan region, helping employees stay on the job and helping employers retain their employees. In his new book, Mark Peters tells the story of how it came into being, why it succeeded, and why it's the model other cities and regions should consider."

—Milinda Ysasi, Executive Director, The SOURCE

THE
SOURCE

USING THE POWER OF *COLLABORATION*
TO STABILIZE YOUR *WORKFORCE* AND
IMPACT YOUR *COMMUNITY*

BY

MARK PETERS

Cover design by ICHD Designs.

Typesetting by Quadrum Solutions Ltd.

For inquiries about bulk purchases, permission to use any of the content of this book, or speaking availability, please email mp@lionrockholdings.com.

Library of Congress CIP data is on file.

ISBN:
978-1-7358950-0-0 (hardcover)
978-1-7358950-1-7 (paperback)
978-1-7358950-2-4 (ebook)

Lion Rock Press

CONTENTS

Foreword. ix

Introduction. xv

Chapter 1: An Eye-Opening Experience. 1

Chapter 2: Picking Up the Reins. 11

Chapter 3: Driving Change, Through Bumps and All 19

Chapter 4: Meeting a Pioneering Engineer with
    a People-Centric Idea 35

Chapter 5: The View from the Roof 43

Chapter 6: Changing Lives 51

Chapter 7: The People Who Make it Work. 61

Chapter 8: A Human Resources Perspective from
    Our Partners 69

Chapter 9: The CEO Perspective: Benefits
    and Recommendations 77

Chapter 10: An Idea That is Spreading 87

Conclusion 95

Appendix I: A Get-Started Checklist 105

Appendix II: A Note About Grant Funding. 109

Resources 113

Endnotes 117

Acknowledgments. 119

About the Author. 123

FOREWORD

Years ago, in my first conversation with Mark Peters, he told me, "Over the years, nonprofits have come to me and asked for money, but they don't ask me for advice. I have to believe the ability of my enterprise to solve problems is greater than the 10 percent of my bottom line that I can afford to give away."

I would come to understand that this was far from a casual remark, but rather a doctrine underlying Peters' approach to business leadership. Business was not set apart from our societal challenges, but rather it could exacerbate those problems – or it could deliver solutions. Peters chose to be on the side of the solution.

In the years leading up to the 2020 Pandemic, corporate America experienced a foreshadowing of what will be a defining leadership challenge for decades – the acquisition and development of talent. Surveys of executives in 2018 and 2019 already pointed to labor availability as the largest impediment to business growth. The prevailing 3.5% unemployment rate had both good and bad implications. To be sure, that low rate represented meaningful job gains in the decade following the Great Financial Crisis. But the unemployment rate calculation has both numerator and denominator, and the latter, the size of the overall labor pool, reflected two trends retarding the growth of our workforce and our economy.

The first trend working against growth was imbedded in demographics, the natural ebb and flow of different ages into and out of working years. The baby boom generation continue to exit the workforce, largely outpacing the entrance of younger people. Needless to say, demographic problems do not lend themselves to easy and timely policy remedies – "fixes" may only impact years or decades later. China's heavy-handed "one child" policy has now caused a significant long-term growth risk for that country, while efforts to boost native population growth, like the Soviet Union's "Mother Hero" program, ultimately encouraged 430,000 women to qualify by raising families with ten (!) or more children. U.S. population characteristics, while not the result of intentional government policy, have had just as profound consequences.

American businesses have luxuriated in the labor resource of the millennial generation, a demographic boom driven by a surge in birth rates that peaked in 1990. Those born in that year are largely in the labor pool, but the supply of native-born workers is falling; by 1995 birth rates had fallen 20% and pre-Pandemic birth rates were 40% below those of 1990, suggesting that businesses will face a permanent talent shortage. The economic and social disruptions of the Pandemic point to further decays in American fertility rates, eroding our future economic potential beyond the worst imaginings of the demographic doomsayers. Even immigration will not solve this problem, as birth rates have fallen across the globe, with notable parts of the developed world not even replacing their existing populations. If "demographics is destiny," the business community is destined to live in a talent-deprived world as workforce growth in many countries will slow or even turn negative.

There is an important caveat to this bleak picture. We can avoid the consequences of a labor shortage if we become better at developing the full potential of our own population. We need a new talent system in our country. This is the opportunity that Peters chose to embrace, sharing his experience with readers. Tens of millions of our fellow Americans have been marginalized from the labor force, a number so staggeringly large it cannot be defined solely as a social issue, but as a critical economic problem as well.

Peters' leadership – and this book – pave the road to the solution: making sure we give every American the path to gainful employment and further advancement. Peters' work is no theoretical model, but the hard-won lessons of a great practitioner. As the CEO of Butterball Farms, a multigenerational family business, Peters well understands the challenges common to privately owned companies and the need to find workable solutions to these obstacles.

Companies like Butterball Farms are the unsung heroes of the U.S. economy. These are companies rarely studied in business schools, rarely featured on the Wall Street-obsessed financial television networks, and rarely profiled in national business magazines and newspapers. Yet, they are hotbeds of innovation and provide the lifeblood of economic activity in countless communities across America.

Peters used his position at Butterball to gain a deep understanding into the broader national challenge of our marginalized workers. His company's experience in "second chance hiring," employing people with criminal records, offered a window into the structural barriers to employing marginalized workers, notably the traditional role and training of human resource professionals. Peters also saw the complexity of the support required to sustain the employment of those marginalized through a lack of financial resources, knowledge, mentorship or because of legal barriers.

Dealing with complexity and barriers is not typically a fit for small businesses – the resources required simply are too costly and hard to scale enough to justify the investment of time and money. The extraordinary story of "The SOURCE" is the way Peters was able to build a collaboration among companies and industries, creating a common vision that would create the scale needed while offering a compelling return on the financial investment.

Our nation is currently wracked by a realization that we have not lived up to our American ideal as a land of opportunity for all. Capitalism and the free enterprise system are under scrutiny, declared by some (largely unfairly) as the cause of this injustice. Even those who do not blame capitalism for social woes question whether our economic system can provide solutions. "The SOURCE" is a testament to the power of the business community – and a visionary leader – to solve societal issues in a way that is not charity, but simply good business. That this mode is "good business" should not be stated with any apology; it means that it can be reproduced and spread widely, with commensurate powerful impact.

For the general public, this story will be a revelation that can redeem capitalism in the public eye. For the business community, Peters' work creates a guide to solving coming labor shortages. Most importantly, for those who have been marginalized from the workforce, "The SOURCE" offers the path to lead lives of meaning and contribution, a foundation of stronger families and communities. It is a model worthy of study and worthy of replication.

Jeffrey D. Korzenik

Chief Investment Strategist, Fifth Third Bank

Author of "Untapped Talent: How Second Chance Hiring Works for Your Business and the Community" (HarperCollins Leadership, April 2021)

INTRODUCTION

This is a book about meaningful leadership—the kind of leadership that succeeds in running a profitable business, and in improving lives: the lives of your frontline workers and, by extension, the community in which you do business. It is the kind of leadership we need now—from a business, economic, social, and, I believe, ethical perspective. It is also the kind of leadership that can only come from business leaders like you.

Of course, there is a long and growing tradition in America of business leaders committing to be a force for good. More than a century ago, Andrew Carnegie wrote: "The problem of our age is the proper administration of wealth, so that the ties of brotherhood may still bind together the rich and poor in harmonious relationship."[1] Believing that wealthy individuals had an obligation to administer their wealth for the benefit of others led him to become one of the greatest philanthropists in history, ushering in the Golden Age of Philanthropy.

By the middle of the twentieth century, the idea spread to organizations with the birth of corporate social responsibility;[2] by the 1970s, there was a consensus among many leaders that business had a responsibility to help solve social problems. The Committee for Economic Development of the Conference Board suggested that it was in the "enlightened self-interest" of corporations to make more substantial efforts to promote the public welfare.[3] After all, they observed, "Business is a basic institution in American society with a vital stake in the general welfare as well as its own public acceptance." Specifically, they argued, businesses have an obligation to provide jobs and economic growth; run their businesses fairly and honestly; and become more broadly involved in improving the conditions of the community and environment in which they operate.

The socially responsible business model—a for-profit business dedicated to a more just and sustainable world—followed. Ben & Jerry's, one of the best-known pioneers of this model, made it clear in their mission statement: they exist to make the world's best ice cream, run a financially successful company, and make the world a better place. More recently, Certified B Corporations have gone even further by committing to create value for non-shareholding stakeholders, such as their employees, the local community, and the environment.

For more than a century, in short, the business leadership community has agreed that it is our responsibility to justly administer resources, treat employees fairly, and serve our communities. The question—in challenging times and in prosperous ones—is *how* do we do all this in a way that makes a meaningful difference by tackling core, systemic problems that affect businesses, employees, and communities?

For more than a century, in short, the business leadership community has agreed that it is our responsibility to justly administer resources, treat employees fairly, and serve our communities.

In the pages that follow, I will tell the story of one successful effort to do all those things, called The SOURCE. But before I tell you about the solution—which can be replicated and has already been in nearly ten states—let me briefly discuss the current three-fold problem it seeks to solve.

Many manufacturing and services businesses have exceptionally high turnover rates that eat into profits and efficiency. The reason for this high turnover is that their workers walk such a financial tightrope that one small setback—a broken-down car, for example—can lead to a cascading number of other problems. Lacking the money to get a car fixed, they can't get to work; because they can't get to work, they lose their job; when they lose their job, they and their families may in turn lose their homes. All of this has a direct impact on the community in which they live, through poverty, educational performance, crime, and more. So, businesses, employees, and communities suffer.

Now, before exploring the solution, let's briefly reflect a little more deeply on that second dimension—the financial tightrope that many frontline workers walk—since it is the pivot point on which turnover rates and negative community impacts rest, and one that will become ever more serious in the years ahead.

FRONT-LINE WORKERS WALKING AN EVER-THINNING TIGHTROPE

A sick child, car breaking down, personal medical crisis, eviction, a utility shut off, mounting debt: these are uncommon experiences for most of us. But for frontline workers, they can be the kind of blow that can jeopardize attendance, productivity, and employment. There are two reasons for this; one is that many are unequipped to navigate—or simply distrust—our complex social safety net system. They don't know how to access help, they don't know who to ask, and they don't trust the sources of help that are available. The second reason is that they lack the financial cushion to withstand these kinds of events.

Consider: even before the recent financial impacts of the global COVID-19 pandemic, low-income wage growth in this country had effectively stalled. From 2000 to 2018, the fiftieth percentile of hourly wages increased from $17.89 an hour to just $18.72—less than one dollar an hour in nearly twenty years.[4] With ever-rising costs, this means they clearly have been going backward.

Now, what of the future? While there is much we can't predict, it is clear that the continued development of automation, robotics, and artificial intelligence will only make the vulnerability of frontline workers a more serious issue in the years ahead. As the *New York Times* reported in 2019: "Automation is splitting the American labor force into two worlds. There is a small island of highly educated professionals making good wages at corporations like Intel or Boeing, which reap hundreds of thousands of dollars in profit per employee. That island sits in the middle of a sea of less educated workers who are stuck at businesses like traditional manufacturing, hotels, restaurants and nursing homes that generate much smaller profits per employee and stay viable primarily by keeping wages low."

Approximately 25 percent of US employment, or thirty-six million jobs, face high exposure to automation in coming decades—with more than 70 percent of the tasks performed by people in those jobs at risk of automation, according to a 2019 Brookings Institute report.[5]

The risk of automation is highest for people in the jobs that now pay the least. And this displacement will disproportionately affect men, young people, minorities, and disadvantaged populations, because these are the people who are working in our production, transportation, and construction sectors.

Automation is also likely to have the most disruptive impact on states like Michigan, that have economies reliant on manufacturing and agriculture. But this is not by any means only about America's home of automobile and other manufacturing. The nineteen states identified as Heartland states have a higher than average rate of likelihood that jobs will become automated.

Now, consider the fact that if low-income workers represented only 5 percent of America's workforce, that would be a significant problem. But low-income workers represent 58.3 percent of America's workforce.[6] That is a massively serious problem with implications for everyone and our economy as a whole.

Businesses pay the price through absenteeism and lost productivity, distracted or unmotivated workers, and the significant cost of turnover. Communities pay the price through increased crime, homelessness, transience in local schools, and a sense of hopelessness. Families pay the price, as these pressures exert enormous stress that can be felt for generations. Taxpayers pay the price because people who are unable to keep up with their bills or pay for groceries turn to food stamps and other forms of public assistance. And clearly, workers (the people working for you and me) pay the most personal, poignant, and profound price of all.

BUSINESS LEADERS ARE BEST POSITIONED TO MAKE A DIFFERENCE

If it is clear that allowing this situation to continue will affect all of us, the question is who can make the critical difference? Non-profits and religious institutions do what they can but don't have the funding capabilities to have systemic impact.

The government already spends billions on efforts to change this situation, to little or no avail. Its work-readiness programs are of questionable value, given the time it takes for the government to approve and deliver new programming and the relative speed of change in our economy.

As business leaders, we need to figure out how to help people get stabilized and move them through the talent system to employers who can pay them a higher wage.

Some have suggested the government should provide every worker with assured basic income. But as straightforward as that sounds, it would be what the poet and farmer Wendell Berry describes as a solution that "causes a ramifying series of new problems." Institute a living wage for all working Americans and the price of most things, like eating out, clothing, lodging, most household goods, education, hospital stays, home healthcare, and medications would rise, since the cash would have to come from somewhere—likely, taxes on businesses and the people still working, which is not a palatable solution at all.

This leaves us: the business sector. As business leaders, we need to figure out how to help people get stabilized and move them through the talent system to employers who can pay them a higher wage. We are the ones who have the ability to create a better pathway for our nation's low-skill and middle-skill workers, and we must take the lead—because we have the most to gain by figuring it out and have the most at stake if we don't.

Ask yourself: What if we could fix it? What if we could set up structures for our employees that would make the essential difference between keeping a job and losing it when something rocks their fragile world? What if we could provide a different kind of safety net, a real-time resource that our low-income workers currently lack so that when life happens, they can keep on keeping on rather than lose everything? What if we could bridge the trust gap and help our people navigate the complex social safety nets already in place that they too often can't or won't access on their own?

It doesn't have to be a hypothetical question. In the chapters that follow, I am going to describe one clear, practical, successful, and repeatable path that you and other business leaders can take, one that will allow you to serve your company, your workforce, and your community. It is based on The SOURCE model that is the result of a unique collaboration between a group of business owners in Grand Rapids. We agreed to cooperate around talent recruitment, retention, and advancement—to see if it worked. And it has.

We asked: Can we do well *and* impact these problems? Can we be financially successful *and* change the outcomes of the people who work for us? Can we collaborate, as a community, even as we compete in the world? The short answer is a resounding *yes*! It has been a journey but along the way, together, we have saved hundreds—maybe thousands—of jobs, changed career outcomes for many, and delivered an average return on investment to partner companies of 200 percent a year. By sharing this story, my hope is that you will see how leading collaboration efforts like this have a positive and sustainable impact on your business, employees, and community.

LEARNING TO BE A LEADER

Before getting into it, let me tell you a little about me. I grew up in American business. My dad was involved in the development of the iconic Butterball Turkey, something many people think about every year during Thanksgiving season when we give thanks for the abundance this country offers. He later sold his intellectual property rights to Swift & Co. but licensed the Butterball name back and started a new venture, appropriately enough, creating premium, specialty, quality butter.

When I took over this family business in 1995, I set out to run it differently than my old-school, curmudgeonly dad. I believed then, and I believe now, that businesses can do well *and* do good. We can be financially successful *and* take care of the people who work for us. We can collaborate in a community even as we compete in the world. My experience has shown that to be true.

We prove every day in our for-profit businesses that we are the innovators, the problem solvers, the value-adders in our economic system. We can solve this problem, too.

Now, I know that you, like me, didn't get into business to address the personal challenges our workers face. Like you, I have spent my life living and working in the for-profit world. But nobody else is going to do it. We prove every day in our for-profit businesses that we are the innovators, the problem solvers, the value-adders in our economic system. We can solve this problem, too.

This book will share the story of how this model solution came to be through my experiences—beginning at the age of twelve—at Butterball Farms, Inc. I sometimes joke that if my father didn't want me to care about people as much as I did, he shouldn't have made me work in the factory from such a young age. But it was this experience that awakened me to the challenges that frontline workers face and gave birth to a determination to be a different kind of business leader. I share all this, and some of my early clumsy efforts, to turn our company into one that was both financially successful and enriched lives. Through this I hope you will see how I learned to be a leader, how change truly happens, and be reminded that temporary failures can lead to positive breakthroughs.

Most importantly, it will also give you a blueprint, a framework any group of businesses and any community can use to address these issues. It will explain how we began, the challenges we overcame, and the successes and failures we experienced. You'll hear from some of the other business leaders involved in our effort, and you'll learn more about how you can implement our approach in your community.

I hope you will read this book with an open mind. Even more importantly, I hope you will come away inspired and with a sense of urgency, as a leader, that you can and in fact must take a leadership role in the talent system you have influence over.

Key idea:

We all know the talent system is broken.
We as employers have the jobs.
Ergo, we have the solution.

Chapter 1

AN EYE-OPENING EXPERIENCE

When I turned twelve, my dad announced that I wouldn't be spending any more summers at our cottage in Holland, Michigan. My only choices were to work in the yard, or work in his butter factory. I chose the yard, but three days later my allergies chose another fate. I ended up in the temperature-controlled, filtered-air environment of a food processing plant, Butterball Farms. My first job was basic janitorial work: sweeping the factory floor, shipping docks, and machine shop, as well as cleaning and sanitizing the restrooms.

On my first day, my dad gathered his supervisors around his desk and introduced me. Then he said, "Even though he is my son, if he does anything wrong, fire him. Don't come bother me. Just fire him."

Clearly, my dad was a genius engineer and an inventor, with sixty patents and three market-defining inventions. But he was not a big-on-social-skills kind of CEO. In fact, I don't believe he cared about his workers or their lives at all; at least, he didn't treat them as if he did.

Unlike my dad, I was mainly interested in the people I worked with. I was also a whimsical, slightly unfocused kid who liked to break the rules. I was sure that eventually I would mess up, so, getting as many people as possible to like me seemed the best way to prepare for the day I would need to talk someone out of firing me.

Getting to know the people who worked in my dad's factory was an eye-opener. I learned that they sometimes had to choose between buying groceries or new school clothes for their children. And that when their old car broke down, they didn't have the money to fix it. They were tired, and they were stressed from having too little money to meet everyday expenses—the kind of stress that wears you down when it becomes a way of life.

The irony was I would hear these stories and then go home to a ten-thousand-square-foot home with eight bedrooms and six baths in East Grand Rapids, with a full-size tennis court out back. I struggled to make sense of the disparity and asked my dad about it. He told me that, in America, everybody had the same opportunity to succeed, regardless of the circumstances they grew up in. They could lift themselves up by their bootstraps. He would tell a story about someone he knew who beat the odds and worked his way out of poverty—as if that proved that if that one person could do it, so could everyone.

But over the years, I became increasingly troubled by how things just didn't seem to add up. I was being raised in a conservative Christian home where we believed everyone was created in God's image, and I lived in a country where everyone was said to have certain unalienable rights. But my friends at the factory did not have equal opportunities, and my father did not treat them as equals. It was clear to me they were disrespected and largely unhappy.

It was a work environment that used people up and disregarded all moral responsibility for how the business may have been contributing to a broken system.

On the factory floor, many people made it only three days before they quit. It was not much better in the office, which was an open floor plan with my father's desk in the center of everything—with every other desk facing away from him. People felt he could be looking over your shoulder at what you were doing at any time, which was often enough to always keep you on edge. He had a penchant for control

3

that was profoundly disempowering; as a result, few people wanted to be there. As one of my Dad's employees said: "Butterball Farms was where you worked while you were looking for a real job."

The older I got, the more the disconnect between my values and the way I saw people treated bothered me. I knew my family was playing a large role in making workers' lives miserable for as long as they could stand working for us. It was a work environment that used people up and disregarded all moral responsibility for how the business may have been contributing to a broken system. Sitting with my sister on the roof of our house one day, I said if I ever had the chance, I would do things differently. I would find a better way to run a business.

THE SECRET CLASSROOM

But first came college. While also working full-time, I enrolled in Calvin College, a Christian college in Grand Rapids. My father had always said that you have to have a marketable skill to be successful. I chose management. "You can't be in management unless you're good at something," he said. "You should become a CPA." So, I pursued a BA in business from Calvin and a BS in accounting from Davenport.

I hated accounting and didn't feel like I was learning much. Then one day my father took me to a business meeting at McDonald's, his biggest customer. The buyer asked if I would like to attend McDonald's Hamburger University, their training facility in Chicago that teaches employees about restaurant management.

"That would be great!" I said.

My father had not planned on this. But he had to go along with it.

It was a fantastic experience: a ten-day intensive program that focused about 60 percent of the time on people practices, such as team-building, conflict resolution, and other talent management skills, and 40 percent on equipment practices, such as how refrigerator systems and shake machines work. It was inspired by McDonald's founder Ray Kroc, who once wisely said: "If we are going to go anywhere, we've got to have talent. And, I'm going to put my money in talent."

I probably learned more about business and management in those ten days than I did in six years of college. And I was so excited about what I had learned that when I came back to work, I wanted to share and implement everything. But my dad wasn't interested.

So, I quietly set up a training room on the third floor, which was primarily used for storage. It was the perfect site for a clandestine classroom. I put in a white board, chalkboard, and some tables and chairs; and I started holding weekly hour-long training meetings with our dozen frontline supervisors in two shifts. I began with the people skills portion of the McDonald's workbook, then moved on to teaching some of the popular management books at the time: *The One-Minute Manager* by Ken Blanchard; the *Fish!* series by Stephen C. Lundin, Harry Paul and John Christensen; and *Games People Play* by Eric Berne.

We did this for about a year without my dad knowing about it. We were having fun and making progress, and I thought it was just what our company needed. Then one day, my dad needed to get his car fixed, and he wanted me to meet him at the dealer to give him a ride back to the plant. He looked for me but couldn't find me. He paged me, and I didn't respond. So, he asked his assistant if she knew where I was. Not one of the people I had befriended, she told him to look for me on the third floor.

"Why would he be on the third floor?" he asked.

"I don't know," she said, knowing exactly why I was on the third floor.

He found me in the classroom and immediately saw what I was up to. He was very quiet but visibly angry, and I always knew that the quieter he was, the more trouble I was in. He ordered everyone back to the plant floor. Then we drove separately to the dealership. On the way back, I kept waiting for him to fire me. But he said nothing until we arrived back at the plant, and he told maintenance to pull everything out of the classroom and padlock the door.

For the next several months, I drove to work blasting Elton John's "The Bitch is Back" telling myself, "I'm not going to let him get to me," and vowing to find a way to resume the trainings. Three months later I cut off the padlock, put the white board and chalkboard back in, and started up again. Only this time, I took the precaution of having an intercom installed so I could hear his pages and respond before he found me.

The second phase of my quiet insurgency lasted three years, and once again, it was working. We were making positive changes in the workplace, in spite of my dad.

THE BEGINNING OF THE END OF AN ERA

Some years later, shortly after my dad turned eighty-five, he had a heart attack. He'd still been working tirelessly. When he was released from the hospital a week later, he told my mother to bring him his work clothes, the khaki pants and khaki shirt he always wore, and then he went straight to the office. He was still prideful and seemed to think he had to continue to model a profound work ethic. But it was the beginning of the end: about eighteen months later, he passed away—and my life, in all ways, changed in an instant.

> **There are three primary reasons why families fail to effectively transfer wealth. Our family checked every one of these boxes.**

Only about 30 percent of family businesses survive into the second generation. Only 12 percent are still viable in the third generation. And only about 3 percent continue into the fourth generation or beyond. According to a study by the Williams Group, there are three primary reasons why families fail to effectively transfer wealth: 60 percent fail as a result of a breakdown in trust and communication; 25 percent fail because there has been no preparation of heirs; and 10 percent fail because the family lacks a mission.

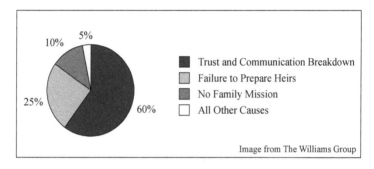

Image from The Williams Group

Our family checked every one of these boxes. My dad never talked about the future of the business. No one had any idea of my dad's intentions relative to the family business or his estate: not me, not my mother, not any of my eight siblings; so we were more than a little anxious to learn what, if any, instructions he left in his will.

The day after the funeral, my mother, my sisters and their significant others, and Frank the attorney, gathered in the sunroom of my mother's house for its reading. My father's assets, Frank said, were split fifty-fifty in terms of value: the house, cottage, and some of the company stock went into a marital trust for my mother; the remaining portion of the company stock went to me. He did not even mention any of my eight sisters.

I don't remember much about what followed except for my sisters' and my mother's clear pain and confusion. How could a father not recognize eight of his nine children? It seemed incomprehensible at best, deeply unkind at worst. At the same time, some of my sisters said: That's just like Dad.

Perhaps to protect me from my family's immediate reaction, Frank said he wanted me to take him straight to the plant before his drive back to Chicago, so we drove to the plant, where I gave him a tour—clueless about what I would soon find out about the realities of inheriting my father's business.

Key idea:

- Our businesses are unintentionally contributing to a broken system.
- We need to be intentional about our purpose.

Chapter 2

PICKING UP THE REINS

As a new thirty-year-old CEO, I had never managed more than my $30,000 annual salary. I had never dealt with attorneys or CPAs or bankers, or seen our company's corporate taxes. Then suddenly, I held the keys to a $12.5 million business. I was so unprepared for the challenge of running a business that I didn't even know it would have been possible to sell it. I was simply plunged headlong into chaos: trying to assure customers and vendors that business would continue as normal, dealing with workers' compensation and wrongful discharge lawsuits, and most worrisome, a $1.7 million inheritance tax bill. I learned that I would somehow have to quickly come up with $350,000 for the first installment.

It would take me about six months to sort through some of these things and get to the point where I could begin to focus on what excited me the most: the opportunity to change the company's culture. This was important to me from an ethical standpoint, but also because our toxic culture had serious negative business consequences. For example, when I inherited the company, Butterball Farms had a turnover rate of 400 percent. Most of the churning was in critical direct labor jobs, which meant we'd often hire twenty people on a Monday, and it was a good week if we had five people left by Friday. As a result, we were routinely hiring an average of three people a day—just to keep eighty positions filled. People would walk out in the middle of a shift, or simply not show up anymore without even bothering to call in.

As a new CEO, I thought: If I just fix the culture and make it a positive environment where people feel valued, they will stay, and our business will take off.

Higher-than-average turnover sometimes comes with the territory in low-skilled jobs; 400 percent turnover is beyond astronomical. It is bad business. The average turnover rate across all industries in 2017 was 3.5 percent, according to the Bureau of Labor Statistics. Across manufacturing, it was 2.5 percent a month. Yet even at those comparatively low rates, turnover can be a very high cost of doing business— albeit one that is hard to see.

For all the years I worked for my father and observed how people were treated, I was certain that the problem stemmed from the negative, even toxic workplace culture he had created. As a new CEO, I thought: If I just fix the culture and make it a positive environment where people feel valued, they will stay, and our business will take off.

I had actually taken my first step in this direction the day my dad died. I went directly from the hospital to the office. Walking in the front door, I passed his big empty desk and the many drafting boards in the engineering area. I went up to the chief engineer and head of procurement and said, "I need to speak with you."

He was one of the two key people who reported directly to my father. He was a dishonest man who had been taking kickbacks from suppliers and was widely disliked for his own toxic way of treating people. I walked into his office and handed him termination documents. "You need to read these," I said. "I really don't care to work with you."

He was angry but not surprised, and I had no doubt it was the right thing to do. There was no way I could change the culture to one that valued people if one of the people at the top not only failed to value those employees but the organization itself.

Another day, I called all our employees together and ripped up my father's rulebook in front of them. This was not a normal employee handbook that explained benefits and general work practices. There were no benefits—at least no health insurance, no 401(k) or education benefits. It was just a twenty-page list of rules that largely stemmed from attempts to prevent recurrences of things that had gone wrong or that he didn't like. It was lazy management. Instead of talking to people and helping them understand his thoughts on best practices, when something happened that he didn't like, my father just added another rule. It declared that people could not, for example, chew gum, and when they could and could not use the restroom and how long they could take. The result: eighty people had to use a restroom that had six stalls in it during a ten-minute break. People hated it for good reason: it oppressed and disempowered them.

Ripping it up in front of them, as I explained, was my way of saying: I am not going to try to be the boss who called all the shots and on which everything depended. Butterball was not going to be just about me and my desires. Everyone now had the freedom and the responsibility to make Butterball a better place.

The next thing I did was redesign the employee dining and break areas—before redesigning management offices—because I wanted to send the signal that the people doing the front-line jobs, who had been most disvalued, were now valued. We set up large well-lit break rooms with sinks and refrigerators and ovens, a locker room and showers along with uniforms and laundry service so people didn't have to pay to clean their own clothes.

> **Ripping up the rulebook was my way of saying: I am not going to try to be the boss who called all the shots. Everyone now had the freedom and the responsibility to make Butterball a better place.**

CHANGING OUR HIRING PRACTICES

Perhaps most substantially, I began to change our hiring practices. Under my father's leadership, people had been brought into the factory in groups of twenty. They were taken on a tour, asked questions as a group, then told they would begin on Monday or "you don't have a job here." It was efficient but there was no dignity to it. People were merely treated as cogs. Nothing conveyed that they mattered as individuals, or that what they could bring to the company was important.

Under my leadership, prospective frontline workers no longer interviewed in a group as if being evaluated as livestock. On the contrary, they met with me, and they met with me before being interviewed by anyone else. I did this because I wanted to send a clear message: the job they were applying for was *that* important—which, of course, it was. The frontline was where all of my financial problems were taking place.

GETTING CLEAR

Soon after, I read *Built to Last: Successful Habits of Visionary Companies* by Jim Collins and Jerry Porras, and decided that we too needed to come up with a company mission statement and guiding principles. To do that, the leadership team and I did what everyone recommends: we went offsite with a consultant and cross-functional team to come up with what we believed to be the best fundamental truths for our company to live out. At the end of a very long day, we came up with something like "Be a worldwide supplier of specialty butter to ... everyone." We also came up with sixteen guiding principles.

I took this list home with me and tried to let it digest, but it didn't resonate with me—at all; and if I couldn't get all of this in my head and it didn't mean anything to me, I thought, how would it ever have any lasting impact on anyone else and actually come alive in the workplace?

So, I decided to start again and called together a much smaller group: Kasey, who headed up maintenance and had helped me when I had conflicts with my father; Kim, our human resources director; and a few other key leaders. We decided that we needed to simplify what we came up with by distilling it into a more meaningful mission statement and set of guiding principles.

Our new mission statement read simply, "Enrich Lives." Those words still get me excited to keep doing this every day. For me, they mean "We don't just want to manufacture a great product. We want to make an impact for our customers, the people we work with, our families, our neighbors, our communities, and hopefully, we can even make a small dent of good in the world."

> **Our new mission statement read simply, "Enrich Lives." Those words still get me excited to keep doing this every day.**

We also shortened our guiding principle list to six:

1. Have integrity in all interactions.
2. Anticipate and address customer needs.
3. Diligently pursue excellence.
4. Promote continuous learning and innovation.
5. Make the workplace an enjoyable and integrated part of life.
6. Communicate openly and honestly to promote effective teamwork.

The fifth principle spoke to me the most, by far. Maybe it reflects a little ongoing rebellion against my dad, but I believe in it. I believe we bring the whole person wherever we go. The work experience is, in fact, part of our lives and only a part of our lives. And I want it to be an additive part of life, not one that diminishes someone.

But before I could even begin to get serious about making that a reality, there were a few surprises in store.

Key idea:

- Every job we create is important.
- Every person we hire is important.
- Every person brings their world with them.
- Every job should have a next job.

Chapter 3

DRIVING CHANGE, THROUGH
BUMPS AND ALL

Within five years of taking over my dad's business, we had
reduced turnover, people were staying longer, and the work
environment was much happier. We had also grown from
a $12.5 million business to a $20 million one. For a while,
everything looked great, but in time another story revealed
itself. While my primary focus had been on improving our
workplace culture, it suddenly became clear that I had been
blind to some very serious financial problems that would
soon threaten us with bankruptcy.

My father had always told me that I was not qualified
to run a business, and at this point, I realized he was right.
In five years, I had basically flipped the company upside

down: from a company that was financially strong and culturally weak to a company that was becoming culturally strong but financially weak.

My father had always told me that I was not qualified to run a business, and at this point, I realized he was right.

One day, I was at my desk with a stack of invoices, writing checks. I came to the invoice from our butter supplier, always our largest monthly invoice, and this one was for $40,000 and due the next day. I always had money to pay for butter when it arrived. But this day, I looked at the balance in my checkbook and realized I didn't. I would have to wait a few days past the due date before I would be able to pay for a shipment. That had never happened before. But I thought it was some weird timing issue, and I kept carrying on, not thinking too much about it.

Then a few weeks later, it happened again. On paper we were making money, we were improving, and we were growing. But somehow, I didn't seem to have any cash. I wish I could say I took leadership and addressed the situation. Instead, I stuck my head in the sand, sure that the little cash problems would take care of themselves.

But about six months later, I saw we'd be out of cash soon. In fact, we were in a rather serious negative cash flow position—not that I knew what a "negative cash flow position" was at the time. (A finance degree would have been more helpful than my accounting degree.)

I called some bankers. The first one to take my meeting instructed me to bring three years of income statements, balance sheets, and tax returns. He reviewed them and asked me questions, and then turned down my request. It turns out that bankers don't really want to lend money to a company that recently went through a change in generational leadership, has questionable accounting practices, one customer that makes up more than 80 percent of the business, and is currently out of cash.

Eventually, I was able to secure the only kind of loan I could in our position: one with a high interest rate. I also had to put up our fully paid facilities, land, and personal property as collateral. On top of that, I had to sign a personal guarantee that if the business could not pay back the loan, I would.

The loan was enough to keep our business operating another year and a half; then I ran out of cash again. I was again struggling to pay our butter supplier on time. If I got too far behind, they would not ship product to me. Then, I knew, we'd be late on a shipment to McDonald's, which is not something you want to do. I grew up with the understanding that McDonald's has an iron-clad rule: "We never run out of product." Run McDonald's out of product once and your relationship with them is permanently altered and often terminated. There's nothing you can do to win back their business. As I sat there and played that scenario through my head, I knew that if we lost McDonald's, we'd be out of business. Worse than that, we would be out of business with me still owing more than $1 million personal debt to the IRS, plus a million-dollar corporate loan to the bank.

I knew the bank was not going to give me any more money. So, in my desperation, I started to think about mezzanine financing, the highest-risk form of debt available to a business, and I called my brother-in-law. Warren had bought and sold companies his whole adult life. You could say he was a private equity guy before it was fashionable. He'd had incredible successes and a few failures—so, plenty of experience. He said he would be happy to help.

Warren is married to my oldest sister and about thirty years older than me—almost my mom's age. He is a large man with gravitas and expertise. We met at his office and then went out to lunch. I asked about mezzanine financing with the hope that he might be willing to put money into the business.

"If you do not want to lose control of your company, do not take any mezzanine financing and do not take on any more debt. Fix your problems."

He said, "Look, if you take mezzanine financing, the financier's goal is going to be to get control of your company and eventually sell it. If you do not want to lose control of your company, do not take any mezzanine financing and do not take on any more debt. Fix your problems."

His message was not threatening. It was measured. Basically, he was saying: Look kid, get your business together, or you're going to lose it. I knew I did not want to lose the business or give up control.

I went home with a sense of panic—and no sense of what to actually do, or how I had gotten into this mess. With all our growth, why was the bottom of our financial statements printed in red ink?

I put my desk on the plant floor, had a phone wired to the desk, and began watching everything to try to figure out why we were losing money, even when our sales were up. I calculated that I was literally six weeks away from running completely out of cash.

Then one night, running numbers one more time, I came to the simple insight that you can grow your business and not make more money. In fact, I realized that our internal operations were so inefficient that the faster I grew sales, the faster I would go bankrupt.

As I sat over the spreadsheets, I tried to figure out how many pounds of butter an employee would have to pack in an hour in order for us to stop losing money and at least break even. I calculated that we produced an average of eighteen pounds of butter per labor hour. At that rate, we were spending more than we were earning. So, I plugged in nineteen pounds an hour. We were losing money. I plugged in twenty. Still losing money. At twenty-one pounds, we were losing money. It wasn't until we got to twenty-two pounds an hour that we would even break even. At twenty-three pounds, we would finally begin to make a profit.

To capture the scale of these numbers, I need to add that because I had approximately 180 employees at the time, the amount of money I was losing per person had to be multiplied by 180. And then it had to be multiplied by the time they worked. The bottom line was we needed to produce $160,000 of additional product to sell every week, without adding any labor—just to break even.

The immediate order of business was to urgently and dramatically improve efficiency. Because of my inexperience at the time, I thought getting from eighteen to twenty-three pounds packed per hour represented an increase of just five points, and would be easy. In reality, it reflected a 30 percent increase in productivity, just to break even. I'm happy I didn't realize it at the time. I may have quit.

* * *

Change had to be made, and fast, but I couldn't afford to hire a consultant or any kind of expert to help me figure this out, and there wasn't time. Then I realized we had all the experts we needed, and they were all around me. So, I got all the team leaders involved and started asking all the people working in the plant for help solving the problems.

Manufacturing businesses can lose money in half-penny increments. It's easy to miss where those losses are, and we had. But now that we were looking, we began to find many sources. For example, we didn't have good weight control on our production lines. Because we wanted to make sure we were not cheating our customers, we routinely erred in the other direction—packing 9-pound cases instead of 8.5-pound cases. In other words, we were giving away a half-pound of butter per box. Then we found our scrap rates were very high. And so on.

Manufacturing businesses can lose money in half-penny increments. It's easy to miss where those losses are, and we had.

I put a new laser focus on production numbers. I required team leaders to call me every hour with production numbers—24 hours a day. I was newly married, and the calls came through the night, which isn't great for any new marriage. But I knew it was that important to saving my business, and I never let anyone off the hook. If they hadn't called me by three minutes after the hour, I would call them.

25

If they didn't answer, I would come down, even at 4:00 a.m. It was important that everyone understood the numbers, and important that everyone understood the commitment.

Perhaps most significantly, I introduced a new incentive program to engage more team leaders in *wanting* to drive change. I gave team leaders an option. They could continue to be paid $12 an hour, or they could take a cut in pay to $8 an hour with an added bonus: for anything produced above twenty-two pounds packed per labor hour, I offered to split the gains with them fifty-fifty. Moreover, they would see their bonuses in real time.

Half the leaders signed on immediately. By the end of the first month, they were making more money than those who hadn't signed on. By the second month, every team leader had moved over to the new compensation plan.

Under the old plan, workers made $35,000 to $45,000 while working sixty hours a week. Under the new plan, in the first year, some of the team leaders made $55,000 in forty-hour weeks. A handful made $70,000.

Our productivity soared. Not only were we able to pay our workers more, but the company was finally showing a profit.

And it worked. Our productivity soared. Not only were we able to pay our workers more, but the company was finally showing a profit.

I didn't do this because I could afford to. I did it because I couldn't afford not to. As entrepreneurs, many of us think we don't have time to work with others to solve a crisis, and that it is better to just do it yourself. But I found that the results of engaging people were irrefutably positive: getting people involved in helping solve the problem accelerated our financial turnaround. In fact, I am convinced it saved my company.

Tying compensation to performance has a number of other benefits, as well—including cutting overtime and workers' compensation costs. In the nutty environment I inherited, we had people working ten-hour days six days a week to meet production goals. And with all the inefficiencies, people were literally running around with coolers full of product. People would get tired, slip, and fall. Or cut a finger while working. But with introducing efficiencies, within a year we eliminated most overtime. People were feeling less stressed, less overworked, and less tired. There were fewer injuries. They were more receptive to trainings. They were happier.

Team leaders could see a direct impact between what they did and what they earned. For the first time, they had some control over what they were going to be paid, and a sense of having a stake in how the company spent money. Butterball was no longer a place you go while you're looking for a real job. It was becoming a great place to work, somewhere people like to be and want to stay, or get ready for the next job. If we had not done the work to change the culture, I don't believe I would have ever earned the credibility and support I needed to turn things around.

> **For the first time, team leaders had some control over what they were going to be paid, and a sense of having a stake in how the company spent money.**

* * *

It was a slow walk out of this financial crisis, but walk out we did. And as we did, I became more committed to diving deeper into what, in truth, excited me the most: my vision— and mission—of enriching lives by helping people.

To do this, I naturally looked to our human resources department for help. Our HR manager was a talented, hard-working woman, but I had come to see that she did not share my philosophy about helping people succeed. I replaced her with a young man named Andrew Brower, just back from the Peace Corps and new to a corporate setting. I shared with Andrew that I truly cared about the people who worked for me, wanted to help them, and was committed to help stabilize those who had challenges that interfered with their ability to get to work, and to help them grow and flourish. I refused to believe that we could not make money and make life better for our employees as well. Or, in the words he recently reminded me I said: "I am committed to the human resources department being a resource for the humans here, which I mean in the truest and fullest sense."

But achieving this goal presented several challenges. First, our plant ran on the thinnest of margins—earning fractions of a penny on each product. If your business runs on thin margins or has negative cash flow or a difficult budget situation, it is likely you will spend money on equipment or marketing—something that is going to hopefully expand the business. It is unlikely you will spend money on improving the workplace culture.

Second, the learning curve for entry-level positions in our factory was quite short. In three weeks, someone could be trained and become as productive as someone who had worked there for four or five years—which meant long-term employees would easily become bored. And third, as in many small- and medium-sized production facilities, there were few growth opportunities. The vast majority of employees were hourly workers on the plant floor, and there were only a handful of coveted positions such as team leaders, maintenance technicians, quality technicians and office support. Most people, especially the more capable and ambitious ones, felt stuck.

> **We needed to figure out how we could provide support and make things better for these good workers with no place to go and plenty of personal challenges.**

We needed to figure out how we could provide support and make things better for these good workers with no place to go and plenty of personal challenges. Payroll was the first thing we focused on. Some assume that low-income workers don't track things very carefully, but that could not be further from the truth when it comes to paychecks. They know what the deductions should be to the penny. We also had some problems with the payroll inherited from my dad's day, so we finally upgraded to a time clock and automated payroll system, which eliminated the problems.

We also decided to take advantage of the fact that people tend to pay careful attention to their paychecks to put information in the envelopes about available support services and other important community information. For example, we contacted local schools to get parent-teacher conference schedules and included them in the pay envelopes to increase the likelihood that parents would attend and get the information that would help them better support their children's education.

More substantially, we started introducing benefits programs that had been lacking under my father's leadership because he thought that things like health insurance and vacation were not worth investing in. People were happy to receive these benefits, but surprisingly, at first many of them did not take advantage of the health insurance to get medical care because they were distrusting of hospitals and other institutions. To help, we added an internal education program to develop their confidence in the medical services they had access to.

When we introduced 401(k) plans, we uncovered a similar distrust—in this case, of banks. Employees actually bragged about having 401(k) plans but didn't take advantage of them; so, we brought someone in every quarter to offer education and encouragement, as well as assistance in how to complete the paperwork. After that, participation went through the roof—and more than 80 percent of all eligible employees were registered for 401(k) plans within two years of our introducing the program.

We empowered employees to make decisions that would benefit them and the company.

We also introduced other new benefits programs, including one that paid employees to take college classes in any subject they wanted, even if it did not relate to our workplace. We partnered with the Inner City Christian Federation—a local organization similar to Habitat for Humanity—so employees could get help in preparing to buy a home and put aside some funds to help them do so by matching the savings they accumulated for a down payment.

Perhaps most significantly, we empowered employees to make decisions that would benefit them and the company. I remember one day when a group of team leaders came to me to say they wanted to add another runner on the plant floor to help move products from one place to another.

"Okay, let's run the numbers," I said. Right then, I went up to the big whiteboard in my office and we ran through what it would cost, what it would save, and the overall impact on the bottom line. Adding a runner, it turned out, would lessen each team leader's weekly paycheck by about $50.

"If you're good with that, I'm good with it," I said.

In unison, they said: "We'll find another way."

Still, I wanted to do more for my employees. There was just something inside me that said, "We can do better than this."

Engaging my leadership team in decisions like this meant they were deeply invested in helping me improve efficiencies and quality. By necessity, I had succeeded in forgoing the cost of a high-paid consultant and found all the support I needed right on my own team.

Still, I wanted to do more for my employees—provide them with more concrete support—even though I still could not afford to pay for it. There was just something inside me that said, "We can do better than this."

That's when we went to see Fred Keller.

Key idea:

- Our HR departments are compliance departments. What our people need is a place to access resources they need.

- Providing benefits is not enough. There are a lot of people who need to understand how to use them.

Chapter 4

MEETING A PIONEERING ENGINEER WITH A PEOPLE-CENTRIC IDEA

Fred Keller has always been a man ahead of his time. When he founded Cascade Engineering back in 1973, he did so with the desire to create a business with a different mindset. That meant, as he puts it today, acting on conscience as much as capabilities; solving problems without creating new ones; innovating with a sense of integrity; and setting new standards for how the world and people are treated. In short, he set out to establish a socially responsible business long before that became a popular thing to do.

Today, with 1,900 employees across thirteen North American facilities and additional operations in Europe, Cascade—which is still headquartered in Grand Rapids—is one of the largest Certified B Corps in the world.

As a child of the 1960s, he told me that he grew up convinced that whatever society was doing was wrong, and if we could figure out how to do it right, everyone would be better off.

At heart, he subscribed to the idea that leadership meant getting the best people and then getting out of their way. He wanted to believe that everybody has great potential—and if he as a business leader could only figure out how to support them, he could help unlock that potential—and wouldn't that be a glorious, fun thing to do?

Then he walked out onto the production floor one day and talked to a relatively new hire name Ron Jimmerson. Ron, he learned, had come off of some social program and just wanted to have a job, a steady job where he didn't have to be dealing with people issues. He wanted to be with himself and not have to worry about other people.

"That's interesting," Fred said. "But, Ron, do you have an interest in doing an experiment with hiring folks on welfare or who are in deep trouble?"

Ron took the bait.

They got a van that employers could sign up for through a Michigan vanpool program at the time and went out and picked up six or eight people from the inner city and brought them to the Cascade plant near the airport. As Fred recalls it, they were all smiles.

Six weeks later, they were all gone. They weren't prepared for the work, and Cascade wasn't prepared for them.

Fred and Ron scratched their heads. They said, "Well that didn't work," and went back to doing their own thing— until sometime later Fred shared what he had tried to do with a friend, Stuart Ray, who owned more than a half-dozen Burger Kings in the area.

Stuart said, "How about a work-to-work program? I will train them up, and when they have been with me for a prescribed amount of time, they'll move to Cascade. It will be good for them and good for me."

Around the same time, Fred also established a welfare-to-work program with the State of Michigan Family Independence Agency, which is now part of the Department of Health and Human Services.

"It was a very good idea," recalls Linda Grund, who was Cascade's Director of Human Resources. "And like any great idea, it turned out that we hadn't thought of everything and we had some situations that didn't go well. We brought in a whole bunch of people, and they were out the door in a very short amount of time.

"What we learned—what hit us in the face—was that when you are bringing people in, you don't just give them fish, you have to teach them how to fish," she continued.

"We had to recognize that people coming in to work for us who had been on public assistance had barriers to employment: they lacked transportation, or daycare, or this was the first job they ever had. Maybe they had spent time in jail or just gotten divorced. The question became: What could we do to help individuals get past those barriers so that they could actually come to work and be successful?"

What they soon recognized was that if a welfare-to-career program was going to work, they would need a state case worker on site.

What they soon recognized was that if a welfare-to-career program was going to work, they would need a state case worker on site. After all, as an employer, there is a boundary between an employee's personal life and work life that must be respected. An employer can't ask: How many kids do you have? It looks like you have an attendance problem. Do you have a daycare issue? And not being able to ask those personal questions would mean not being able to get to the root of the problems that were affecting someone's work performance.

But a caseworker with the State of Michigan could ask those questions—and, as a result, could help solve them.

So they brought one in—paying the state for a case worker named Joyce Marsh to be on-site five days a week from 7:30 a.m. to 3:30 p.m. Then all the human resources department, or a supervisor, had to say to an employee who was struggling with showing up at work was: "Maybe you should go see Joyce. She can help."

Of course, not all supervisors would be inclined to even point an employee in the direction of getting help. Sometimes an employee would show up late and attempt to explain by saying, "I got beat up last night," or "My car wouldn't start this morning," and the supervisor would say, "That's not my problem."

But Fred and Linda responded by instituting training for all supervisors to help them understand Cascade's commitment to helping workers succeed and how simple it would be to say, "Let me go get Joyce." They also had to teach people in the organization to ask enough questions to send them to Joyce. So, Cascade trained all supervisors and managers—exposing them to training by Ruby Payne, the educator and author best known for her book, *A Framework for Understanding Poverty*. This helped them understand how to more effectively transcend cultural differences and other communication barriers—and, most significantly, help supervisors spot potential trouble spots and refer workers for support.

The impact was dramatic: monthly turnover went from 40 and 50 percent to 3 percent. "We all had high turnover then—and now—because the economy is good," Linda told me. "And turnover costs are high. It is higher the higher level the person is. But even for a production operator, it costs thousands of dollars in turnover costs when you lose a person—and that is thousands of dollars from the bottom line."

BUT HOW CAN A SMALL COMPANY ACT LIKE A BIG ONE?

After Fred was gracious enough to allow Andrew Brower, my new human resources director, to observe how Cascade was supporting its front-line workers, Andrew was excited. He had watched new employee orientations, walked the floor with line leaders, and learned from the executive team running human resources. He saw clearly that they had an intentional plan around retention, plus a stair-step process to help employees advance. There was no guesswork. Everyone knew that if they developed certain sets of skills, they would earn higher wages. As a result, almost by default, they were cross-training themselves and preparing themselves for when a new position would come open. That opportunity to earn more if they learned more was creating a highly dedicated staff. In a word, he said, it was outstanding.

But there was a catch. As Andrew put it, "They're a $250 million company. We're a $25 million one. How do we keep up? It's a different ballgame for a company our size."

He was right, of course. Now we had to figure out how a small company like mine could act like a big company like Cascade.

> **Key idea:**
>
> - Most of our companies do not have the financial resources to act like the big companies we compete with. We must figure out how to act like a big company especially when it comes to our talent.

Chapter 5

THE VIEW FROM THE ROOF

The Butterball factory is wedged in the middle of an industrial ghetto filled with old, dingy, and well-used brick and steel factory buildings. There is no beautiful architecture. No five-star restaurants. No downtown hustle and bustle. If you go up to the roof, however, you can see the entire skyline of downtown Grand Rapids. It's where I go sometimes when I need to sort out something truly difficult—and it was where I went one day to chew on the question that was nagging at me: How could a company like mine develop the clout and resources to help people the way Fred Keller was doing at Cascade?

When you are inside your own building, you often think your problems are unique. But very often, they're not.

Usually, when I am on the roof puzzling something out, I look out at the distant skyline. But this time, I found myself focused on the buildings that were within a half-mile radius of us. All of those buildings, I thought, had to be filled with people like the ones working in the factory below me. People struggling to make ends meet. People worrying about how to pay their rent and how to keep their homes warm. Those personal challenges, I thought, had to interfere with their ability to work, just as they affected the people who worked for me. And it had to be affecting the businesses' bottom line through lost productivity and high turnover. So I wondered, what were these other employers doing about it? When you are inside your own building, you often think your problems are unique. But very often, they're not.

Soon after, I set out to meet with the HR departments of my neighboring companies. I learned that their employees, indeed, had struggles similar to the ones that the people who worked for me were facing. They also had similar aspirations. While the HR people really cared about the people in their organizations, they just did not have the time or resources to do what needed to be done. Employers in our industrial corridor were not directly helping. This was disappointing but not surprising. After all, helping employees with personal problems that interfere with their work life was not—and still is not—part of the mental model most of us have as business leaders. It is not a cultural norm—at least not yet.

Moreover, there was not a clear roadmap for how to help. Most human resources departments aren't set up to handle employees' personal challenges. They spend so much of their time keeping our businesses out of trouble, they have little or no time for anything else. What's more, even if they had the time, they would not be able to ask the kinds of questions that they would have to ask to help resolve personal issues without violating employees' confidentiality.

Most human resources departments aren't set up to handle employees' personal challenges.

Then one day I had an *aha!* moment. I knew that Grand Rapids was full of organizations designed to help people in need and providing exactly the kinds of services our employees needed—and that these organizations had trouble finding clients. They knew that people in need were out there, but the people in need often didn't know that they existed or feel comfortable reaching out to them.

What this meant was that to help our employees, we didn't need to reinvent the wheel. We simply had to connect the dots—to connect our employees with those service providers.

The operative word here was *we*. While Butterball, like the companies led by most of the people I was speaking to, is relatively small, if we joined together around our common need, we would have more power in numbers. We could, in effect, collectively act like a big business.

The trick would be finding people willing to join me in this mission to do some good.

By now, Fred Keller had become a true friend. When I explained my challenge to him, he agreed to work with me to try to bring Grand Rapids business leaders together to explore the idea of figuring out how to enable small companies like mine to have the clout of a big company like his. The general idea was that if we could pool our resources to create an intermediary organization that could connect frontline workers to the services they needed, we would all benefit.

If we could pool our resources to create an intermediary organization that could connect frontline workers to the services they needed, we would all benefit.

We wanted this intermediary organization to connect people with resources that could help them overcome the primary barriers to stable employment, identify continuing education opportunities, buy a first house, and all of the rest of the everyday struggles people face. We wanted this to be a source for tax preparation, wellness, language classes, you name it. We wanted our organization to link everything together to find the right help for the individual and family.

Together, Fred and I identified sixteen CEOs who we thought would be good candidates for this venture, and we invited them to the Peninsular Club, a more-than-century-old private club in downtown Grand Rapids better known as the Pen Club. We made our pitch, doing our best to paint a picture of the value of providing the services that would lead to a more stable workforce.

Of course, something like this was going to take some capital to get it up and running. Every CEO there, I knew, was writing checks to support a variety of nonprofit causes. They were not afraid of spending money. So I asked them to each commit $500 a month for a year to make this happen. As Fred recalls, most of them sat there with stern faces, their arms folded, and didn't say a word.

Then one raised his hand and said, "How did you come up with that number? I mean, we have Bob's business over here and he has three hundred employees, and I have fifteen. That doesn't seem quite fair that we should each pay $500."

Knowing he had a point, I looked at him and said, "I understand. But I also know that every person in this room can afford $500 a month for twelve months to see if it will work."

By the end of the meeting, eight CEOs said yes. With that, we had a budget and a beginning. We also thankfully received some funding from the Grand Rapids Community Foundation, so we went ahead and made Andrew Brower the first executive director of our new organization. We named it The SOURCE.

Andrew recognized that one of his first challenges—to keep those eight CEOs committed beyond the first year and attract more businesses to this effort—would be to not only provide the help to frontline workers that we envisioned but to also create effective ways to convey the true value of this work to business leaders.

"CEOs and executives are usually very smart people with a certain set of experiences, but rarely are their experiences what a lot of entry-level workers have experienced."

As he put it, "CEOs and executives are usually very smart people with a certain set of experiences, but rarely are their experiences what a lot of entry-level workers have experienced. They know how to solve problems. It would be unthinkable for them to quit a job because their car breaks down, or they have a childcare issue."

He realized that part of his job would be to help business leaders recognize that helping create stability in the lives of their workers would benefit them through reduced turnover costs—but also that the lives of many of their workers were quite different from their own, as were their needs. To grasp the value of this experiment, they would need to understand something about that, too.

Key idea:

- Our Human Resource Departments can not do this, nor should they.

- When we collaborate with other businesses, together we can act like a much larger enterprise.

Chapter 6

CHANGING LIVES

What happens when a tragic accident occurs just when a smart young woman graduates from college and is ready to take the world by storm? Or when a young man who grows up in a tough neighborhood, makes a series of bad choices that land him in prison, then gets out and tries to course-correct but finds the odds against him? If we are honest enough, we recognize that every day there are countless "there but for the grace of God go I" stories unfolding, many in our backyards or under the rooftops of our businesses.

The following stories are of real people, whose names have been changed for their protection. They are a snapshot into how unstable many people's lives are and how we often have no idea when we meet them in our workplaces. They also show how an organization like The SOURCE can have a life-changing impact at critical moments to help people get back on their feet and contribute to their employers and communities—by offering services we sometimes describe as those of a trusted and knowledgeable friend.

COMING BACK FROM
A DEVASTATING ACCIDENT

When Anna graduated from college with a degree in digital marketing, she and her friends interviewed for jobs in Kalamazoo. "We were going to go there to kill it," she recalls.

Every day there are countless "there but for the grace of God go I" stories unfolding, many in our backyards or under the rooftops of our businesses.

Then she was in a boating accident and broke her neck.

"I was a single woman who wanted to do the American dream. I thought I had it all mapped out. But then my whole path shifted," she says.

Unable to work, save occasionally as a substitute teacher, she became homeless and lived out of the back of a camper, then squatted in a friend's basement where she said she was becoming as welcome as a dead fish. "I was suicidal. The pain was so bad I would vomit for fourteen hours straight. I put on a bunch of weight.

"Finally, it got to the point that I was going to be a shut-in or run with it and secure employment on a permanent basis."

She volunteered at a Veterans Affairs office to gradually build up strength. Then she heard about someone known as a great supervisor at Spectrum Industries, a member of The SOURCE.

"He knew that I hadn't been working a lot. He knew money was tight," she says. He also knew that she needed to get a pair of $150 shoes for her position but didn't have the money for it.

"He connected me to The SOURCE, and within days they made things available," she says, lifting her leg to the table to show off her shoes.

"There are a lot of nonprofits in Grand Rapids but there are so many hoops you have to jump through. It's almost a full-time job getting access to what you need. The SOURCE gave me access right now. It was amazing.

"They also kept following up. They wanted to know my story. I told them about having been homeless and my dream of owning a home. They connected me with a loan officer and a realtor. And I got a mortgage for $365.09.

"I was a little hot mess. Now I am anchored into the community in homeownership. I'm invested. It comes from being at a company that is part of The SOURCE," she says.

"They are angels," she adds of the people who work at The SOURCE. "They hold you with so much dignity. They show you matter, you count, you're visible."

Until her accident, she reflects, she thought life was easy. She has learned it can be very difficult indeed—and that sometimes any of us might need someone to pick us up.

"Someone said The SOURCE is there if you make bad choices. I think The SOURCE is there to break down barriers and empower you," she says.

IMMIGRATING TO SUPPORT HER CHILDREN

Gabriella came to the United States in 1989 because she could not earn enough in her home country to support her four children, who ranged in age from two to nine. Leaving her children in her mother's care, she found her way to Butterball Farms in Grand Rapids, where she landed a job and began sending money back home.

But when employee hours were later reduced because demand was down, she found herself in trouble again. "I was talking with a coworker about making ends meet," Gabriella recalls. "She said go to The SOURCE. They can help you claim unemployment."

It would be the first of many times The SOURCE provided critical help that kept her working. When her car was stolen, they helped her recover it. When she had to have brain surgery, they helped her communicate with her doctors; and, because she was concerned about whether being out on medical leave would jeopardize her job, they helped her get to work whenever she was able. But what she is most grateful for is that The SOURCE reunited her with her daughters.

"I had a lawyer in San Francisco who was helping me do all paperwork and then somebody must have sued them. They disappeared. I was trying to get in touch with them and couldn't," she says. She tried other options but could not afford them—even the $300 to get a single piece of paper translated.

At The SOURCE, Erika Gonzalez handled it all at no cost. "It is thanks to Erika my daughters are here now. She feels like an angel. She is a person in life I will never forget.

"Every time I walk into The SOURCE, I feel at home. You can just tell that the people who work here want to be here and they want to hear you."

"I love this place," she adds. "They are my family, they have helped me with everything, really everything. Every time I walk into The SOURCE, I feel at home. You can just tell that the people who work here want to be here and they want to hear you."

STARTING OVER

Aniyah is a forty-two-year-old, smart, ambitious, flawed woman. She used to earn more than $100,000 buying and selling houses in Chicago. Then she was charged with defrauding the government for failure to pay property taxes. Suddenly, everything fell apart: she was a felon, divorced, out of work, out of money, and responsible for four children.

"It was a bad time. My sister had just died of cancer. The felony was not something I had planned."

She moved to Grand Rapids, remembering from an earlier trip to Michigan that life seemed more affordable there. In Chicago, to let her son play flag football would cost $500. To let her daughter become a cheerleader cost $1,000.

Michigan seemed like it presented more options and freedom for her children. And, as she recalls, "I wanted to give my children a different experience from what I had."

She reached out to a women's shelter to get temporary housing and moved—landing an entry-level job as a machine operator with Cascade Engineering.

When she began, she was on public assistance because 25 percent of her salary was being garnished by the IRS—leaving her with too little to provide for her family's food, shelter, and other necessities.

Then someone told her about The SOURCE. They got on the phone with the IRS, reviewed her case with them and found she did not, in fact, owe as much as the government had said she owed, and reduced her tax obligation by more than 50 percent. They helped her complete all her tax forms. Eventually, they helped her get off public assistance.

As Aniyah puts it, "Cascade is big on helping people get off public assistance. And they changed my mind about it. I wouldn't get back on assistance now. It's embarrassing."

With more stability, she also started to advance on the job—rising from a Level A15 position as a machine operator to a C18 position as a supervisor, and she plans to continue to do what it takes to keep moving up.

"I think every company should have something like The SOURCE because you want your employees to come to work stress-free."

Her children, she says, are also thriving—participating in the debate team, the chess team, volleyball, and track.

"I think every company should have something like The SOURCE because you want your employees to come to work stress-free," she says. "You want them to be looking out for your product. Now that I'm not worried about the IRS, it's easier for me to do my job and do it efficiently."

FROM HELPED TO HELPER

After she graduated from high school, Alejandra started working at DECC, a second-generation family business that has been named to *Inc.* magazine's 5000 List of America's Fastest Growing Private Companies. Her plan was to work for one year to save enough money to go to college. It didn't work out that way.

She had a baby and then another and soon found that her entry-level factory job did not pay enough to support a child, let alone go to college. She came to The SOURCE for help applying for food stamps and Medicaid.

What she soon discovered was how different dealing with someone from The SOURCE—called Resource Navigators—was from dealing with a case worker at the Department of Health and Human Services.

"The SOURCE gave me the ability to become a better person."

"With the DHHS, you don't know who your caseworker is. You don't build a connection. They deal with a lot of people, and they don't remember your name," she recalls. "This was so different. You see the same faces. They know your name. You don't have to explain your case all over again."

They helped her apply for assistance—and they also told her about a program that would allow her to go to college. As a first-generation college student, she had no idea how to sign up for classes, so they went with her to do it. Now she continues to pursue her college degree part-time. Along the way, they also encouraged her to apply for an opening at The SOURCE.

"My goal when I started working here was to offer the same experience I experienced: to feel like this is a safe place to talk about problems and no one is going to say, 'Oh, you're doing it wrong.' My goal is to not judge and not make assumptions because there is always something behind what you see people do. It's like, 'Okay, you made a mistake. Now let's make it better.'"

"The SOURCE," she added, "gave me the ability to become a better person."

Key idea:

- What happens in people's lives outside of work impacts how things get done at work.

- Senior leaders rarely understand the life struggles of their workforce.

Chapter 7

THE PEOPLE WHO
MAKE IT WORK

Broken lives are complex, and restoration is a journey. It takes a special kind of person to step into those lives and help make that journey easier. Erika Gonzalez, Managing Director of The SOURCE, exemplifies that kind of person.

She is, to begin with, nobody's fool. It's true she has made the kind of difference in hundreds of people's lives that leads even some of the most hardened men and women to call her a miracle worker. But, as many clients of The SOURCE have learned, you'd be mistaken to try to fool her. If she is going to dedicate her formidable talents to helping someone navigate a personal challenge that is interfering with their work life, they'd better be telling the truth, they'd better be dedicated to doing their part to right their situation, and they'd better be ready to keep it up.

An immigrant from Mexico, Erika, unlike many of the low-wage workers she helps today, did not grow up in poverty. "My father managed a construction company, my mom was a special vocation teacher, and we had a maid," she says. "But I was taught that social status doesn't matter—that everybody is the same, and we need to help each other. And my family modeled that belief."

One of the more influential early experiences that, in retrospect, seems to have prepared her for the work she does today was the way she spent afternoons after school. "Before I was old enough to stay by myself, my dad would pick me up from school and take me to Mom's work for the afternoon. I would play hide-and-seek with deaf people, people with Down Syndrome, people with speech problems. It gave me a lot of empathy and taught me how to communicate across differences. I learned that if someone was deaf, you had to pat them on the shoulder."

As the oldest child in a family that prized independence, she also learned to be a problem-solver in a variety of circumstances that gave her the courage and confidence to take on almost any challenge. Today, although she is in a leadership role, she continues to work directly with clients because, she says, she loves not only helping people but also the challenge of becoming something of an impromptu expert on a wide range of issues that front-line workers find themselves facing—without a clear idea about how to resolve them.

"We are their best friends who know how to solve things," Erika says. "Whether a client's challenge is about taxes or unemployment or fixing their credit, we know what to ask to navigate the system. Many of our clients just don't know how to do that." This is what is at the heart of it: a trusted, knowledgeable relationship.

Indeed, many front-line workers who consult The SOURCE have experienced their share of racism and discrimination. As a result, they don't trust "the system" so they don't engage with it, which means when they are in a crisis, they can find themselves stuck between a rock and a hard place. Their peers, who they do trust, don't have the knowledge to help them, and they don't trust the organizations that could.

But when they come to The SOURCE, they find, in Erika and her colleagues, people they feel they can trust who can also help them navigate the necessary systems. It begins, she says, with establishing trust—through genuine empathy. After all, most of the situations people come for help with are not situations they are likely to feel proud about. The challenges can range, at their most extreme, from having a criminal background that makes it nearly impossible to find adequate housing, to being homeless because they simply do not have the skills to earn enough money to cover their living expenses.

Many front-line workers have experienced racism and discrimination. They don't trust "the system" so they don't engage with it.

"I try to not make them feel bad about what happened," Erika says. "They feel my empathy. And then they begin to trust me to be on their side."

As Mindy Ysasi, Executive Director of The SOURCE, says: The SOURCE team strives to create a respectful, hospitality-like experience—which is quite different from what many people seeking support experience from social service agencies.

RESOURCE NAVIGATORS

One key to this is the use of resource navigators. These talented, highly knowledgeable folks come into the factories of The SOURCE member companies, meet with our employees in our facilities (often on company time), and help overcome a fundamental problem of mistrust that many employees feel toward the government, or banks, or leaders, or their employers. Or they may have experienced discrimination or racism and be wary that they will be mistreated again. So, when they need help, they often are reluctant to turn to (or may outright refuse to consider) the very agencies and institutions that could most help them. And yet their peers, who they do trust and will turn to for help, don't have the knowledge or expertise to be effective.

In a resource navigator, employees get to relate to someone they see all the time and can get to know over a long period. Resource navigators aim to establish trust through genuine empathy and by focusing on solutions, not judgments.

Here is a sampling of cases across the top six issues our resource navigators encounter:

- **Housing**. An employee was homeless because his felony background made it difficult for him to secure housing, and his wife was pregnant. He came to The SOURCE, where they called several property management companies and found one that would accept someone with a felony. They helped him fill out the application, found funds to pay the application fee, and helped him apply for DHHS benefits to get assistance that would enable him to pay his first month's rent and deposit. The employee and his wife were able to move into a new apartment before their baby was born, and he is now maintaining stable employment.

Resource navigators aim to establish trust, through genuine empathy and by focusing on solutions, not judgments.

- **Finances.** Because he was behind on his bills, another employee's water had been shut off, and he had just received shut-off notices for his electricity and gas as well. In addition, his checks were being garnished due to back-debt. The SOURCE found a community agency where he was eligible for funds that would enable him to have his water turned back on, and helped him apply for DHHS assistance to cover his other past-due utility bills. They also filed a motion to reduce the weekly payments owed on the back-debt to keep him from getting into the same situation again. He was able to return to work and keep up with his bills.

- **Food assistance.** An employee found herself in a bind, not having enough money to pay for groceries but earning more than the government limits to be eligible for food stamps (total family income of $1,307 for a family of one; $2,665 for a family of four). The SOURCE found a pantry the employee had not known about that was within a half-mile of her apartment. The employee was able to use it as a stopgap to cover grocery needs that she could not afford to pay for at the supermarket.

- **Education.** An employee didn't have enough money to pay for school supplies and the required uniforms for her daughter. The SOURCE contacted the daughter's school and arranged a meeting where the employee was able to get the necessary school supplies. She also found a sale on uniforms and purchased two with community funds and gave it to the employee, who felt relieved that her daughter could start school with all the essentials.

- **Health.** An employee's father had a stroke, which left the employee supporting himself and both parents. He'd bought a house so they could all live together but was having trouble coordinating the move with all of the medical equipment and improvements that needed to be made to accommodate the father's medical condition. The SOURCE connected them with the nonprofit Home Repair Services, where they were eligible for a free ramp. They also were able to meet with a housing counselor to ensure that the new house was affordable. One member of the family also had certain diet requirements and was having trouble using their food stamps to get appropriate food, so the caseworker found a food program that helped.

- **Transportation.** An employee and his wife had only one car but worked in different cities and had to bring their child to daycare every day. As a result, they were both having difficulties showing up for work every day. The SOURCE helped them create a budget and apply for a bridge loan to buy a second car, which dramatically decreased their travel time and eliminated their attendance problems.

Of course, not all challenges front-line workers face fall neatly in one of these six categories. As with most issues any of us face, the challenges cut across several different lines. For example, one employee was suddenly granted custody of his young daughter—and needed help setting up everything that anyone in such a situation would require. The SOURCE helped him get her clothing and things for her bedroom, and arranged before- and after-school care so he could continue to work. They also helped him apply for DHHS benefits and worked with him on buying a car so he could manage getting his daughter to school and himself to work.

Key idea:

- All people need "Trusted and Knowledgeable" relationships.

Chapter 8

A HUMAN RESOURCES PERSPECTIVE FROM OUR PARTNERS

Your HR team is focused on the things that happen on company time and administering available benefits. They aren't able to solve your employees' non-work issues any more than you are—but employees are even more likely to bring these issues and questions to HR than to executives.

It's probably not a surprise that our HR professionals have been thrilled to be able to refer employees to The SOURCE and its resource navigators. They see the results in increased retention rates and healthier, happier employees.

Here are some specific insights, from a few of our member companies.

HERMAN MILLER

Herman Miller is a more-than-century-old furniture store headquartered in Zeeland, Michigan that has created signature modernist products including the Noguchi Table, the Marshmallow Sofa, and the Eames Lounge Chair. Today, their furniture is carried in stores across the nation, including the Museum of Modern Art's Design Store in New York City. They are also a global company, with five thousand employees in the United States and three thousand in other countries. And, like other forward-looking companies that have become member businesses of The SOURCE, they have roots in leadership that recognize the benefits of supporting its employees.

HR professionals have been thrilled to be able to refer employees. They see increased retention rates and healthier, happier employees.

As the story goes, back in the 1930s there was an accident in the factory that resulted in the death of one of the employees. The founder and CEO, D. J. De Pree, went to visit the family. While he was there, he learned that the man had been a poet. It struck De Pree that there was so much he didn't know about his workers—and that he wanted them to be able to bring their whole self to work.

"It was way cool to do that back in the 1930s," says Heather Brazee, Director of Employee Benefits and Well Being for Herman Miller, "and it has always been embedded in the culture. With me being responsible for employee well-being over the last ten years, it became more apparent as I listened to employees and felt empathetic to their struggles that we have to acknowledge that what is happening in one part of life affects every other part of life."

The catalyst that led them to join The SOURCE and make the benefits it offers available to its employees was an "Unmet Needs" survey they conducted to see which kinds of benefits employees valued most. "We can't do everything," Brazee says, "so we thought instead of us deciding what they need, we should ask our employees."

When they did the survey in March 2018, she says, it was almost like a switch was turned on that helped management recognize something that went beyond what they initially sought to find out.

"We weren't ignorant of the fact that there were issues employees were struggling with," she explains. "But we thought, 'We're Herman Miller, one of the best companies to work for. Our employees can't have problems.'"

What they learned was that they did. Says Brazee: "We heard stories about people trying to manage daycare changes, employees without a support network, being worried about their health, finding the healthcare industry difficult to navigate, and fears related to being part of the sandwich generation taking care of both parents and kids. And, managing debt was a big one."

Three months later, Herman Miller joined The SOURCE. Because they are a large employer, they have also trained all their team and manufacturing leaders in the benefits that are available so they will know what they can refer employees for—and how to do it. "With a company our size, it's very difficult for us in Benefits to know that Mark on the floor is struggling with a housing payment or has a shut-off notice," says Brazee. "We don't know those things to be able to recommend him to call The SOURCE before it's too late. So, one of the most important things for us was to get to the people who have these relationships and would be able to recommend The SOURCE."

Unlike other member companies, Herman Miller is also outside Grand Rapids, so they have a resource navigator come on-site twice a week.

"She sits in the common area to help visibly remind people she is there for them," says Brazee. "Usually someone comes up because they are reminded on their break about the benefits of The SOURCE. Lucia talks briefly with them and then sets up a meeting to help."

"Being seen as an employer that is empathetic and really focused on what is happening in employees' lives is important to help us maintain our brand as being an employer of choice."

It creates more of a family feeling at work. "Employees feel more valued and prouder to work here," she says, adding that it also reduces turnover and improves productivity. With Herman Miller now entering their second year as a member company of The SOURCE, Brazee says she can also see the benefits from the perspective of a talent retention strategy. "It is difficult to attract and retain talent because of the market now. But being able to be seen as an employer that is empathetic and really focused on what is happening in employees' lives is important to help us maintain our brand as being an employer of choice."

SPECTRUM HEALTH

Spectrum Health is a not-for-profit, integrated, managed care healthcare organization based in West Michigan that has received America's 50 Best Hospitals Award 6 years in a row from Healthgrades. They have 31,000 employees; 4,200 physicians and advanced practice providers; and a health plan with one million members served in 2018. They are a $6.5 billion enterprise that includes 14 hospitals and 230 ambulatory sites. In short, among member companies of The SOURCE, they are a behemoth. So why, with the kinds of resources they have, do they think it worth joining this effort?

"It's a pretty fascinating story of how we got involved," says Kevin Vos, Senior Director of Hospitality Support Services. "Over the last seven years, Spectrum has pivoted to doing a different type of investment in their employees."

The change began, Vos says, when Spectrum noticed that more than 70 percent of its senior leadership team was aged fifty-five or over. "The leadership said: We need to solve for this, or we are going to have a gap in talent."

So Spectrum first partnered with a local university, Grand Valley State University, to create an accredited executive MBA program that enabled employees to earn their master's at no cost, in part during work time. Vos was part of the inaugural class of twenty-two, earning his degree in less than two years by attending classes on Saturdays and two Fridays a month.

With an eye on the coming talent problem Spectrum sought to solve, they paired the professors with Spectrum executives to design the curriculum. All case studies were also healthcare-based. When it came time for the students to complete their capstone or thesis project, they were instructed to solve for problems in the healthcare industry.

Four or five capstone projects a year were presented to the senior leadership at Spectrum; and one of them, in particular—called Healthy Jobs, Healthier Communities—got their attention. "The project recognized that we had a significant number of entry-level jobs but were not respecting the talent that they had and helping them through a respectful process to remove barriers to employment and career advancement," Vos recalls. "It also recognized that to do this would help the community; and if done correctly, could start solving the workforce gap with their own employees."

Vos was, at the time, in a leadership role in nutrition services which (with the environmental services division) had 1,200 entry-level employees, the most organization-wide. "My boss said, 'You are a leader that gets the bigger picture. Now you need to take that capstone project and do something to implement it.' "

The goal, said Vos, was to "create a program that developed and engaged staff in a meaningful experience that essentially increased their skill level, so they could be promoted and paid more."

Around the same time that he was given this new responsibility, he began to hear about The SOURCE and, in his words, became a "huge advocate" of Spectrum Health becoming a member organization.

"They have been an integral partner in helping us develop these programs because they have more expertise in helping this population," says Vos. "In fact, we just renewed our contract for a third year."

CASCADE ENGINEERING

Cascade Engineering joined The SOURCE a little bit later than most of our other members—because they, after all, had their own program before The SOURCE was even up and running. But ultimately they too joined after recognizing that they could deliver the same benefits at a lower cost by doing so.

Peg Olds, Human Resources Manager at Cascade, said this about the benefits they currently experience as a result of being a member company of The SOURCE: "Costs are down. Quality is up. Engagement is up with employees contributing to make the organization better because they have better ideas. There are a lot of upsides and I actually don't know any downside. It just feels like the right thing to do."

Key idea:

- Collaboration can create expertise none of us can afford on our own.

Chapter 9

THE CEO PERSPECTIVE: BENEFITS AND RECOMMENDATIONS

You might expect human resources teams to like an initiative like The SOURCE. You also would probably expect employees to appreciate it. You might even predict that line supervisors would see the benefit of being able to direct their workers to a place that could help them solve the personal problems that are interfering with their work.

But there's one group you might reasonably expect to be a tougher crowd to convince of the value of a collaborative program like this one: namely, CEOs, who must carefully weigh costs and benefits, and what's best for their business. With that in mind, I convened four CEOs who were founding members or early supporters of The SOURCE to discuss what business case, if any, they see for it: Fred Mellema of the DECC Company, Leonard Slott of Vi-Chem Corporation, Kevin Bassett of Spectrum Industries, and Jay Dunwell of Wolverine Coil Spring Co.

They identified ten clear benefits—some of which surprised me—and offered five recommendations for those considering such an effort in their communities.

TEN BENEFITS

1. **The SOURCE provides financial savings as a result of lower turnover costs.** "Our turnover has gone way, way, way, way, way down, which is great," said Jay Dunwell of Wolverine Coil Spring Co. In fact, since 2003, the average return on investment for member companies has been more than 200 percent of their annual investment.[7]

2. **The SOURCE has improved the workplace culture.** "Employees remember how you treated them," said Dunwell. "When things get good, they'll be the first ones looking to jump ship and go find somebody [another employer] who's going to be more loyal or responsive [to them]. This is a long-term cultural stake we're putting in the ground. I love it when I hear a newer employee say, 'I didn't know that employers could be like this. I didn't know there were places like this to work.'"

3. **The SOURCE solves the confidentiality issue that often prevents employers from helping employees in need.** While personal issues are often at the heart of workforce instability, many employees don't want to share their personal problems with their employers, and employers don't have the right to pry into their employees' personal lives. The SOURCE helps fill that gap by being a third party that employees can go to get help—and still keep their personal lives personal.

> **"I love it when I hear a newer employee say, 'I didn't know that employers could be like this. I didn't know there were places like this to work.'"**

"Now they go to The SOURCE, and it's completely anonymous to us," said Leonard Slott of Vi-Chem Corporation. "The SOURCE obviously knows who they are, but we don't know. We just get a monthly report, saying we saw three of your people or ten or your people or whatever, but there are no names."

4. **The SOURCE is efficient.** Employers don't know all the different social service agencies in their

communities, what they offer, or how to navigate them. Nor do they have the time or inclination to learn about them. But the staff at The SOURCE knows, making it an efficient one-stop solution.

5. **The SOURCE's wellness screenings help workers live healthier lives.** "When we started this up, I had no idea how many people didn't have a personal physician," said Fred Mellema of the DECC Company. "In my family, you always had a doctor. "When we started doing blood pressure and cholesterol screenings, one of the guys on my team's numbers were off the chart," he continued. "He got sent to the hospital. Turns out, he was eating unhealthy food all day, and had a family history of chronic heart disease. But he got on medication, found a doctor, became a regular patient, and is living a much better, much healthier life."

6. **The SOURCE provides better and more varied training than what employers could provide on their own.** "For us, training is probably one of the easiest things to identify as a cost," said Bassett. "So, with The SOURCE, the motto we have is if one of the member companies says they have a need for training in something, we get a trainer and we have a specific training, and offer it to all the other companies to maximize the training spend."

We also found that we were able to engage local colleges in supporting the programs. And, frequently, we find all or a substantial portion of our costs covered by grants. "Many times, we've found some grant money that we didn't even know existed," said Slott. "So, now you have a group of individuals coming together to do this training in one place and it is paid for or significantly offset through grant money. You'd never do that as an employer, right?"

7. **The collaborative nature of The SOURCE allows small companies to act like big ones.** Small companies simply can't compete on their own and offer the kinds of benefits larger companies do. But working together through The SOURCE allows them to do so.

8. **The SOURCE leads to unexpected collaboration benefits.** Collaboration, initially focused on ways to help employees, quickly grew to benefit the manufacturing side as well.

"What else can we do? How can we pull together? What are the common threads between the companies?"

"None of us are experts at everything," said Slott. "So once, Fred [Mellema] had an issue with some powder coating, and I sent my Ph.D. chemist over for the day to help him out with whatever issue he was having." It was just one example of how forming relationships with "neighbor" businesses could help.

9. **The collaborative nature of The SOURCE leads to effective brainstorming.** "The thing that I've always appreciated about The SOURCE and this group of CEOs is that we're always trying something different," said Bassett. "We've had different initiatives, but it's always, what else can we do? We know we still have more issues. What else can we put together? How can we pull together? What are the common threads between the companies?" This collaborative and innovative nature is what enables the initiative to continue to progress.

10. **Collaborating through The SOURCE helps foster career paths.** "If you have somebody that is a superstar in your organization, the supervisor often doesn't want to give them up," said Mellema. "Or, we just find another spot for them internally. But is that really best for the employee? Not always."

The SOURCE allows employers to identify career paths between companies, or across the entire community, that keep talented workers engaged. (In fact, coordinating progression across multiple companies holds such promise, it will be the subject of my next book. Stay tuned!)

In short, while people new to something like The SOURCE often first ask about its financial benefits, what was so illuminating about my conversation with these founding CEOs is that they saw the business benefit to be in the impact on workers and the workplace culture. When you have workers who are happy and want to stay, are better-trained and more-productive, and can find more satisfying career pathways, it leads to a significant reduction in unplanned turnover and increased retention. They also simply do better work.

RECOMMENDATIONS

Ready to get started? Or at least begin exploring the possibilities? Great! Here are five core recommendations:

1. **Make sure you are doing it for the right reasons.** "Identify your culture," said Mellema. "What is the culture of your company? What is it that you are trying to present to your employees on a weekly, monthly, yearly basis? Because if it's just about the bottom line, it's not going to work for you. You have to actually care about the employees."

2. **Identify like-minded CEOs in your community.** "If enough CEOs talk about their employee base or their ability to change lives in their community,

people will listen," said Dunwell. "You need like-minded CEOs desirous of having a positive impact with their employees."

3. **Identify (or become!) the champion.** You need a leader who will instigate, organize, make the initial calls, and provide the time and energy to bring their colleagues together.

"It really has to have a champion. That would be my biggest recommendation," Bassett said.

"You have to find somebody who has the passion for this particular activity," Slott added. "You need that person to go to each CEO and chat each one up personally, give them the 'we need to do this' speech. That person will get the CEOs on board."

> **"If enough CEOs talk about their employee base or their ability to change lives in their community, people will listen."**

4. **Identify key partnerships, such as local social service agencies and nonprofits.** All agreed that having caseworkers embedded is essential to the success of The SOURCE. "You need the caseworker

component, DHS and non-DHS caseworkers, coming into your building," said Dunwell.

5. **Finally, consider ways to fund the initiative**. When we started The SOURCE, we funded it in two ways. First, to have some skin in the game, we asked each member to contribute $500 per month for twelve months. Now, the initial fee is $3,000 for the first year—which is usually long enough for a company to understand what The SOURCE offers, and enthusiastically renew its membership at a higher cost.

We also pursued philanthropic funding at the beginning. In our case, the Grand Rapids Community Foundation generously extended a three-year grant. This was helpful covering initial start-up expenses, and also as a signal to the CEOs involved that the effort would pay off long-term. As it happened, we used the grant funds in the first year, took just two-thirds of the funds in the second year, and by the third year had grown membership dues so much that we returned that year's entire grant.

Summing up, Dunwell said: "The successful businesses long-term tend to be those that are compassionate toward their employees and passionate about their success, [rather] than those that are just after the quick buck."

If that describes you, I hope you'll take the next step—and join what has become an idea that is already spreading across the nation.

Key idea:

- Big learning: We CEO's love our stories. Especially if it is about people in our organizations being successful.

Chapter 10

AN IDEA THAT IS SPREADING

We are not alone in recognizing the challenges our employees face and stepping up to the plate to help them. Employers are slowly catching on.

There are other examples of business leaders and groups of employers, in cities and regions across the country, coming together to identify common issues and formulate solutions.

While I'm proud of The SOURCE and all the employees we've helped over the years, the programs and services we offer aren't a magic formula. I don't believe there's any one right answer when it comes to this kind of collective effort. The issues your city's employers and employees face may be a little bit different than those we face in my city, and so your priorities, partners, and solutions may vary too.

So let me tell you a little about a few related efforts in other communities, and the models they've used to great success:

WORKING BRIDGES

Several years ago, in Burlington, Vermont, the local United Way chapter held a community-wide training on poverty. Executives from a number of prominent local employers attended and learned about generational poverty and financial fragility. These leaders immediately connected these issues to the very real workforce problems they had long encountered—losing employees who could not find childcare or were dealing with substance abuse. Employers convened their own conversation, and soon after, three of them jointly founded an organization they called Working Bridges. They identified employee needs and retained the United Way executives to facilitate the work.

In its earliest days, the leaders of Working Bridges looked to the same source of good ideas that we did when starting The SOURCE: Fred Keller's Cascade Engineering. Working Bridges adopted the on-site resource coordinator concept and chose to fund a position housed within the United Way chapter.

To help employees facing financial issues, Working Bridges partnered with a local credit union to create access to a new low-interest "income advance" loan, as well as financial literacy training and income tax preparation services.

The regular employer convenings have continued and are the source of most new solutions and services offered to employees.

GrOW

In some communities, pre-existing employer groups and organizations, which have long been active in promoting business and serving as a social convenor for local businesspeople, are now experimenting with collective employee assistance programs. For example, recently the Greater Omaha (Nebraska) Chamber introduced a new program for its members, the Greater Omaha WorkLab (GrOW), which leverages the work of an embedded facilitator to provide one-on-one support services to employees of member companies.

Services through GrOW include such crucial programs as help navigating debt; counseling and resources around childcare; behavioral, communication, and interpersonal coaching; addiction and substance abuse program navigation; and other issues that often lead to absenteeism and job loss. Intervention and assistance demonstrably reduce turnover in member companies. This initiative is a partnership with WorkLab Innovations (more on WorkLab below).

In some communities, pre-existing employer groups and organizations are now experimenting with collective employee assistance programs.

CONNECT FOR SUCCESS

In the Seattle, Washington region, employers can access workforce support from a nonprofit called Connect for Success. Connect for Success also follows the WorkLab model of an embedded facilitator and attracts new employer "members" by promising improvements in retention, attendance, and the effectiveness of existing benefit programs. The facilitator is positioned as a neutral, non-HR resource, and employees are pointed to the facilitator to solve their non-work-related challenges.

The nonprofit entity is the hub of this model; employers do not convene or control what services will be offered. Rather, individual employers are more in the role of clients, served by the nonprofit. A different model, for sure, but to the individual employees who Connect for Success helps, it is no less effective.

WORKFORCE CONNECTION

In Cincinnati, for over two decades an organization called Cincinnati Works has provided services directly to residents and employees. In 2017, Cincinnati Works launched a new initiative, called Workforce Connection. This new initiative flipped their traditional model: rather than serve individuals who seek out services, Workforce Connection seeks direct relationships with employers in the region and embeds a facilitator on-site at participating companies.

The services provided are similar to those Cincinnati Works has long provided. But by bringing the facilitator's expertise onto the worksite, employees can far more easily learn about resources and solutions without missing work time.

Again, this model places the nonprofit at the center, serving many business clients.

WORKLAB INNOVATIONS

After studying the Cascade Engineering approach, and then the collective effort that became The SOURCE, the founders of WorkLab Innovations formalized the primary strategies and created what it calls the "Sustainable Workforce Model." The key to this model is an on-site facilitator, present and active within the employer worksite and easily accessed by employees. The on-site facilitator, which WorkLab calls a "resource navigator," meets individually with an employee, assesses what training or services might be most helpful to address issues in the employee's personal life, and connects the employee with the needed training or services.

The importance of this neutral, on-site facilitator can't be overstated. Rather than having shop supervisors or the

HR team try to deal with the many and varied personal and financial issues employees present, an experienced, neutral facilitator familiar with a wide array of possible training programs and available social services can be a far more efficient and cost-effective option. WorkLab resource navigators generally have deep knowledge of local and state nonprofit and social service agency offerings related to housing, transportation, food assistance, childcare, career and financial coaching, mental and behavioral health, and legal needs. Individual employees can and do have long-term relationships with their resource navigators, well beyond what a supervisor or HR representative would be capable of providing.

An experienced, neutral facilitator can be a far more efficient and cost-effective option.

WorkLab Innovations has initiated new affiliated programs in a number of communities nationally. The organization has also identified a number of entities (including The SOURCE) with generally similar approaches and created a loose network for these entities to collaborate, share best practices, and improve their offerings.

* * *

With The SOURCE, we started by getting business leaders together, then built out a joint services offering based on the common problems we were facing. And that's the solution I am suggesting to you.

As shown above, though, some communities are coming at this issue from another direction: a nonprofit takes the initial lead, and then one way or another gets business involved. Frequently, the nonprofit's efforts are funded by a local philanthropy, and the nonprofit then seeks out companies to provide services to (including an embedded facilitator). The end result is often similar to our experience: what begins as an effort to help employees, increase retention, and reduce turnover, gradually becomes a statement of values and a spark to company culture.

With the strong warning that nothing is free—that it is crucial that the employers involved have skin in the game from the very beginning—approaching these issues through the leadership of a nonprofit or a prominent local philanthropy can and does work.

It is crucial that the employers involved have skin in the game from the very beginning.

I've offered you our story and a series of steps for you to follow to replicate The SOURCE in your community.

But if a nonprofit or funder already exists and is willing to act as convener, by all means take advantage of that head start!

Key idea:

- You do not have to start from scratch.

CONCLUSION

I began this book—and my career—determined not to be my father's kind of CEO. I wanted to be a business leader with heart. I have learned so much as a result including, ultimately, from my dad.

A month before he passed away, we went to a food show at Disney World. Disney, which had been one of our largest customers for years, used to invite all their suppliers to promote products to their culinary folks. At the end of the show, Dad said he wanted to go to the Magic Kingdom, which would involve a lot of walking. I suggested he get a wheelchair. He was dead set against it, but I prevailed.

We left the Contemporary Hotel, where we were staying, and took the monorail to the park entrance. Dad said he wanted to go to three rides: The Hall of the Presidents, The Magic Carpet Ride, and It's a Small World. The guy at the ticket counter said, "You know, those are all at three opposite parts of the park. It's nine, and the park closes at ten. There's no way you're going to make it."

I leaned down and said, "Dad, what do you think?"

He looked at me and said, "Yes, let's go for it."

And we did—making it to all three rides, with me running and pushing my Dad in his wheelchair.

As we were coming out of the park, we encountered the closing parade. It was a truly magical experience: the lights, colors, fireworks, dancing. It was amazing, and I looked down at my dad and saw him smiling with tears running down his face. It was one of the very few times in my life I saw anything like that emotion—that heart—in him.

Several weeks later, he fell and landed back in the hospital. It was clear we had entered a final chapter. I told my mom that I was not going to leave the hospital and asked her to get a letter I had written to my dad that he had not yet seen and bring it to the hospital. My father was always critical of my writing, so I felt a bit vulnerable, but I got up the courage to read it.

"Dad," I read, "you have been my greatest friend and my worst enemy. You have held out hope for my success and a supportive hand when I was at my last wit. You have pushed me when others would have settled for what results I had produced. In your own quiet and constant way, you have held me to a high standard—so much so that in many respects it is now my standard for myself.

"Other times I have fought with you and cursed you. There are many times, especially when it has come to matters of the heart, you and I have not seen eye-to-eye. This has caused a long and difficult rift in our relationship, yet we have maintained our friendship."

As he lay silently in his hospital bed, I continued:

"For myself, I face the possible loss of my father with a great and unspeakable sadness. I feel like the best friend I have ever had is slipping out of my life. I fear I have not lived up to your standards, and that I may never be able to. I long for your hug and your smile of approval. More than anything in my life, I have strived for your approval. For the smile or the word that let me know I pleased you or did something well by your standards."

When I finished reading, my dad put his arms out. I fell into his chest, and I finally got the hug I had always wanted. I just lay there and cried for a little while. I don't remember much more of that evening, other than that I ultimately slept in a little family room down the hall from his room.

Then, around three in the morning, I heard my father from his room calling out: "You find my son, I know he is here somewhere."

I immediately ran to his side and sat holding his hand for the next couple of hours. At 6:00 a.m., I called my mom and said, "I don't think Dad's going to be alive much longer." Thirty minutes later, he quietly passed away. For a man who lived with so much force, I had expected some kind of punctuation mark—like a roar. It was more like whisper, just quiet. But the fact that I was there, that I was able to read the letter, get his hug, find a resolution in our challenging relationship, changed my life. It also helped me recognize the truth that we grow by coming up against challenges; and as we grow, we often discover the best in ourselves, the best we have to contribute.

* * *

There is something much more significant—and promising—at stake in all this than my personal story, of course. Namely if we, as the nation's business leaders, do nothing to meet the challenges faced by the people who come to work for us, especially given our knowledge that robotics and artificial intelligence will displace hundreds of millions of workers in the decades ahead, we will be victims to an economic and social system gone awry. And of this you can be certain: Our failure to act will come back to bite us through the almost certain likelihood of increased poverty and the loss of talent development, which will be essential to keep the American economy robust in an increasingly competitive global market.

If we, as the nation's business leaders, do nothing to meet the challenges faced by the people who come to work for us, we will be victims to an economic and social system gone awry.

Let's not be victims to this result. Rather, let us insist on tapping our great capacity as problem-solvers to help create more stability and growth for the people who come to work for us—and then help them take the next step in their careers, for our own collective good. After all, as important as it is to create more stability for workers in times of crisis through something like The SOURCE, it is not enough. We must also help people grow their talent and the collective talent of the American workforce.

That may sound like a tall order—especially because we are not very strategic about talent development or career planning in this country. Think, for example, about the prospects for a young frontline worker in your business. Chances are he or she can learn their job and, in a matter of weeks, become as productive as someone who had worked there for four or five years. Chances are also that there are few places for them to go and grow—say, into one of the few coveted positions as supervisors or office workers. Then what happens? Most people, especially the more capable and ambitious ones, will become bored and stuck. Of course, it is not just the case at your business or mine.

There is a whole population in our country that doesn't ever get unstuck. So much energy and potential are trapped, much like water behind a dam. But if we, as business leaders, can see the benefits of releasing that energy and potential, and if we as business leaders can use our unparalleled abilities as problem-solvers, then we can create better workplaces and a better economy for all of us.

~~~~~~

We can create better workplaces and a better economy for all of us.

~~~~~~

As a businessman, I am excited by the opportunities I see in these gaps. But to make the most of them, I believe we need to own up to a radical fact: that in today's dynamic economy and fast-changing marketplace, we need to be more than employers; we also need to be informal educators who help prepare people for their next jobs even as they execute their current ones.

Is there any question that continuous employment and continuous education are needed in today's economic environment? There is no question in my mind: not if you take the big view that looks beyond immediate quarterly profit results to what is coming down the pike in our businesses, communities, and the global economy in the face of the continued growth of technology and competition; and not if you consider the absence of any system that now effectively serves people and businesses by helping develop and coordinate talent for the years ahead.

So, what specifically do we do to develop talent? Answering this question is beyond the scope of this particular book. First things first, after all: we need to help create more stability for our least stable workers so they can maintain their current jobs; *then* we need to look to helping them take the next step.

But here is a preview of what I believe is needed to grow this kind of intentional talent development. First, we need to change employer expectations: employers need to look at providing education along with employment. If you came to work for me, for example, I would say you have to continue your education to keep your job. I think we have to do this to stay relevant.

We need to create more stability for our least stable workers, so they can maintain their current jobs.

Second, employees need to change their expectations. The expectation has to be that skills will only last three to five years. And third, we need a coordinating organization— because mapping people's education and their careers in our complex, fast-changing world is nobody's core competency.

The goal of such a coordinating organization would be to create a network of employers interested in talent mapping so they have a clear idea of future needs. The value to individuals would be in designing that long-term career strategy so they can always be employed and always get their continuing education. Imagine the tremendous economic power and opportunity for everybody.

If this kind of forward-thinking collaboration sounds like what has been referred to as "a disruptive innovation" then perhaps that is just the kind of innovation we need for the good of our talent system, our businesses, and our economy. In Grand Rapids, we already have begun to take this next step: advancing from a focus on retention to a focus on career progression for front-line workers and creating a talent pipeline that is also shared among employers. The good news is that it is working here. And it can work elsewhere.

My hope is that you find yourself curious enough to learn more—and then take action.

As business leaders, we are some of the best problem-solvers there are. But to really tackle these issues across the nation, we need more forward-thinking, collaborative leaders to step forward. My hope in writing this book is that you find yourself curious enough to learn more through the example of The SOURCE and other organizations listed in the Resources section of the book—and then take action.

Together, we can have a tremendous impact in our workplaces and communities. We have the power and the influence and, I believe, the responsibility to do so. But above all, we have the opportunity to not be victims of a negative story we already see being forecast. The story of The SOURCE demonstrates what is possible, and it can expedite your success because it offers a model to follow. So acknowledge that there is nothing holding us back. Let's take control, as the leaders and problem-solvers we are, and get this job done. There is a dam of potential waiting to be unleashed.

Key idea:

- Don't be a victim. Join me in creating change in the talent system!

APPENDIX I:
A GET-STARTED CHECKLIST

❑ Identify the nature of your own commitment to helping your employees

    ❑ Have you ever thought, "I wish I could do more to help my employees with the problems they encounter in their personal lives?" but feel that your hands are tied?

    ❑ Are there specific issues you seem to hear about regularly (like childcare, transportation, financial shortfalls, healthcare, etc.) and feel compelled to try to address?

    ❑ Are you curious about how other employers deal with these issues?

    ❑ Would you be interested in supporting an external resource to help your employees?

- ❑ Would you interested in exploring whether it's easier to do this along with others?
- ❑ Does your workplace culture allow taking action, even if it doesn't necessarily lead directly to increased profits?
- ❑ Are you okay with keeping value inside the system, so as to give your employees more stable lives?
- ❑ Identify and partner with like-minded CEOs in your community
  - ❑ Would you consider taking a colleague or two to lunch and exploring the common issues your employees appear to face?
  - ❑ Would you consider convening a group of CEOs and fellow business leaders to discuss these common issues?
  - ❑ Are there existing organizations or institutions that could convene these kinds of conversations (local workforce development board, family business center, philanthropy/foundation, Goodwill, etc.)?
  - ❑ Would you consider convening a community discussion group around a single workforce-related topic?
  - ❑ Who will be the champion, who will lead this effort (at least initially)?
    - ❑ Is there a person interested in taking this on?

- ❑ Is there someone within the business community with a reputation for treating employees well? With credibility as a business leader? With credibility and experience as a convenor?
- ❑ If not, is there a small group or committee that might take the lead in convening the initial conversation and activity?
- ❑ Identify and solicit funding
    - ❑ Is there a local funding source that can be approached?
    - ❑ Is there a community foundation or local philanthropy that might be approached to provide initial grant funding?
    - ❑ Is there a large local business that might be interested?
    - ❑ Is there a large local institution, such as a university, that might be interested?
    - ❑ What will the initial and annual contributions of member employers be?
    - ❑ Finally, see the extended note about grant funding below.
- ❑ Identify (and hire) an executive leader, once the funding stream is in place
    - ❑ This executive will facilitate: What are the most important employee issues to be addressed collectively?

❑   This executive will partner: What are the service providers, social service agencies, nonprofits, etc. suitable for addressing these specific issues?

❑   This executive will manage: What are the logistics of providing services? Where will they be provided? What staff will be needed? etc.

APPENDIX II:
A NOTE ABOUT GRANT FUNDING

Don't take the money—it's not free! I have a picture in my head of this great comic where a family is driving down a city street and there is a sign saying "free puppies" with a picture of four cute puppies. The next frame says: That Puppy's Not Free and goes on to list various costs like food, vet, and grooming. As any pet owner knows, there are great benefits to owning a pet, but there are great costs, too.

I have always been the voice at the table saying employers should pay the full cost of this work. I have been convinced since the beginning there is true value in doing the work that The SOURCE does for our companies. Reducing turnover and stabilizing our workforce has real value. If that is true, then someone should pay for the value; since the value is attributed to us (employers), we should pay for it. I had a belief that by getting someone else to pay for the work, the organization would not be sustainable. I have done enough work in the nonprofit world to have seen grant money, usually on a three-year cycle, do all sorts of good—for a short period of time—then when the funding goes away, the nonprofit ends up begging for funds it rarely raises, then having to downsize, re-organize, or worse: start to restructure its programming to chase funding. This common cycle ends with many nonprofits doing work that is out of scope of their mission—or in business terms, not aligned with their core competency.

I was so convinced that what The SOURCE was doing was so critical and had so much impact that we—the founding businesses—could not allow that to happen. We had to understand, every year, the true cost of running The SOURCE, and we had to be prepared to fund the entire cost. So, on the spectrum of voices around the table, I was always the least in favor of "taking the money" from outside funders. I was concerned that if we took too much funding, when it stopped coming the shock of the cost of continuing the work would cause employers to quickly stop participating. This is, in fact, what happened with some WIRED funding that was granted to Michigan in the mid-2000s. One community that received this federal grant funding got the work up and running, but at the end of the three-year cycle, the employers (who had said they would pay when the grant was over) decided it was too expensive to continue.

If the work is to be sustainable it has to create value the employer partners see and are willing to pay for from the very beginning.

There are benefits of not being grant-funded. As members of the non-profit, you and your colleagues can keep the organization very focused on the needs at hand—stabilizing and educating your workforce. You can also track accountability better. As an employer member, you are not going to keep paying if you are not getting a value. Since this accountability happens on an annual basis, the staff stays focused on doing the work you need to have done, instead of going out to look for ways to spend a lump sum of money. Also, if the staff of the organization does not have to spend a lot of time raising funds, they can spend that time solving problems. I recall that we once had an executive director at The SOURCE who sat on another nonprofit board, and when he went to meet with a potential funder for that organization, he was asked about what he did. After describing what he did, the funder asked him why he had never approached them to fund The SOURCE. His response was that he didn't need the money. The funder was surprised, and said she wished more nonprofits could say the same.

All of that to say that I have changed my point of view on grant funding—somewhat. Grant funding can be very helpful to start an organization like The SOURCE, or to fund pilot programs that you would like to test. However, I still believe if the work is to be sustainable it has to create value the employer partners see and are willing to pay for *from the very beginning.*

So, if you are serious about doing this work and building sustainable system change, be careful about how you accept funding assistance. I remain a skeptic. That puppy's not free!

RESOURCES

The SOURCE
Grand Rapids, Michigan
https://grsource.org

Connect for Success, Cares of Washington
Seattle, Washington
https://www.caresofwa.org/employer-services
https://connectforsuccesswa.org

WorkLife Partnership
Denver, Colorado
https://worklifepartnership.org

Working Bridges, United Way of Northwest Vermont
Northwest Vermont
https://unitedwaynwvt.org/workingbridges

**The SURGE Center, Goodwill Industries of
Greater Detroit**
Detroit, Michigan
http://www.goodwilldetroit.org

**Workforce Innovations, Greater New
Orleans Foundation**
New Orleans, Louisiana
https://www.gnof.org/what-we-do/program-areas/workforce/

Retention Plus, OAI, Inc.
Chicago, Illinois
https://oaiinc.org

Workforce Connection, Cincinnati Works
Cincinnati, Ohio
https://cincinnatiworks.org

Team Up, Northern Virginia Family Service
Northern Virginia
https://www.nvfs.org

Achieve Solutions, Towards Employment
Cleveland, Ohio
https://www.towardsemployment.org/achieve-solutions/

Greater Omaha WorkLab, Greater Omaha Chamber
Omaha, Nebraska
https://www.omahachamber.org/resources/talent-workforce/
greater-omaha-worklab/

Mark Peters — Author
www.lionrockholdings.com
mp@lionrockholdings.com

ENDNOTES

1. "The Gospel of Wealth," by Andrew Carnegie.

2. "Corporate social responsibility" was coined by Howard Bowen in his book, *Social Responsibilities of the Businessman.*

3. *Social Responsibilities of Business Corporations.*

4. https://www.epi.org/blog/average-wage-growth-continues-to-flatline-in-2018-while-low-wage-workers-and-those-with-relatively-lower-levels-of-educational-attainment-see-stronger-gains/

5. https://www.brookings.edu/opinions/americas-broken-dream/

6. https://www.bls.gov/opub/reports/minimum-wage/2017/home.htm

7. We calculated this using an average cost of onboarding and training a new factory worker multiplied

by the number of workers The SOURCE assisted divided by three. The idea here is that three touch points typically equaled one job saved since most employers said that after three negative incidents, an employee would be likely to lose his or her job.

ACKNOWLEDGMENTS

Several years ago, my friend and mentor Greg McCann suggested that I write a book. I laughed—politely, of course. But Greg, as he is prone to do, kept nudging—encouraging and eventually persuading me to tell the story of The SOURCE. So, my first thanks go to Greg for not giving up. I also want to thank Lisa Bennett, who worked patiently with me for a year to help distill the mountains of stories, interviews, and research that went into the book you now hold in your hands. Thanks also to Jeffrey Korzenik, Chief Investment Strategist for Fifth Third Bank, for introducing me to Tim Brandhorst of the Law Offices of Marc J. Lane, P.C., in Chicago, who helped me with the publishing end of this process.

I also want to thank so many good people who have contributed to the success of The SOURCE over the years:

business partners, nonprofit partners, government partners, foundation partners and, of course, staff and clients. Every single person who touched this project helped it be what it is today. That said, I would be remiss not to explicitly name the following.

First and foremost, I want to thank Fred Keller for his pioneering leadership. He literally paved the way for The SOURCE; and I know if he hadn't done what he did at Cascade Engineering, The SOURCE would never have happened. Thank you also to Cascade's Executive Vice President Kenyatta Brame; Ron Jimmerson, President and Co-founder of Seeds of Promise and former Senior Human Resources Manager for Cascade; and Dave Barrett, Director of Talent Development.

My appreciation also goes to Andy Zylstra, former director of the Kent and Allegan County Departments of the Michigan Department of Health and Human Services—a courageous and innovative government leader who played the vital role of bringing the Michigan Department of Health and Human Services into this collaborative; and to Randy Kookekee, who kept it going and brought schools to the party.

Hearty thanks to Andrew Brower, now a program officer with the W. W. Kellogg Foundation and previously my guy on the inside both at Butterball Farms and The SOURCE. Andrew contributed extraordinary perseverance, innovation, and a respectful, helpful collaborative spirit to everything he touched. Also Milly Chavez, The SOURCE'S first DHS caseworker, without whose understanding of what we were trying to do and her dedication to it, The SOURCE would likely have not survived past its first year.

I'm grateful also to the late Tina Hartley, who led Goodwill Industries of Greater Grand Rapids and took a chance on The SOURCE and let it be organized under Goodwill's 501(c)(3) before it became an independent organization of its own.

A heartfelt thanks to the companies that bet on The SOURCE when it was just an idea and invested their money and time in getting it off the ground: the DECC Company, Hekman Furniture, Keeler Brass Company, Keeler Die Cast, Michigan Wheel, Notions Marketing, Pridgeon & Clay, and Spectrum Industries. Special thanks also to Fred Mellema of DECC and Kevin Basset of Spectrum Industries, both of whom have been special champions and supporters of The SOURCE.

Heartfelt thanks also to Milinda Ysasi, the current Executive Director; Erika Gonzalez, Managing Director; and the two Joyces: Joyce Rohrer and Joyce Gutierrez-Marsh. They are all hard-working, passionate people dedicated to helping others.

Two other special people without whom this never would have gotten off the ground are Daidre Derzaph, my executive assistant, and Carrie Link, my assistant and community relationships coordinator. Both have daunting jobs to do and put up with my belief that I can accomplish anything and everything at the same time.

Finally, thank you to all who are named in this book and agreed to be interviewed for it.

ABOUT THE AUTHOR

Mark Peters is the Chief Executive Officer of Butterball Farms, Inc., which was nationally recognized as one of The Best and Brightest Companies to Work For® from 2018 to 2020. The second-generation family business, based in Grand Rapids, Michigan, is America's leading producer of culinary butter and margarine and creates custom butter flavors for some of America's biggest brands.

Peters began as a factory worker in his father's company at the age of 12: an experience that taught him first-hand about the challenges that frontline workers face. At 30, he took over the company, determined to lead a financially successful business that would also enrich the lives of its workers.

In 2003, he organized a pioneering group of CEOs and community leaders to found The SOURCE, a not-for-profit organization that has helped hundreds of workers navigate personal challenges that were interfering with their jobs and delivered an average annual return on investment of 200 percent to its partner organizations.

This West Michigan-based model has been replicated in nearly 10 states; and Peters is currently expanding its mission to help frontline workers not only maintain their jobs but progress into better positions within or across partner companies.

Recognized by numerous companies from Ernst Young to McDonalds for his leadership, Peters is an engaging speaker and storyteller who has addressed TEDx and other audiences. He lives in Grand Rapids with his daughter and dog and is an avid boater, biker, and skier (water and snow).